NEW ROYAL COOK BOOK

NEW ROYAL COOK BOOK

ROYAL BAKING POWDER COMPANY

ISBN: 978-93-89582-42-0

Published: -

LECTOR HOUSE LLP
E-MAIL: lectorpublishing@gmail.com

NEW ROYAL COOK BOOK

BY

ROYAL BAKING POWDER COMPANY

THE NEW ROYAL COOK BOOK

The new Royal Cook Book has been prepared to meet the large and ever increasing demand for a guide to wholesome and palatable home cooking. The young housewife will find here complete simple directions for making delicious cakes and other culinary delights. Experienced cooks and those more skilled in the art will find here many of their favorite recipes and in addition helpful suggestions, especially in the matter of saving eggs and other expensive materials.

Every recipe has been tested many times and all have been found excellent.

Royal Baking Powder is used in all recipes in which a leavening agent is required, and the biscuits, muffins, griddle cakes, doughnuts, cakes and pastry prepared by its use are unequalled in texture and healthfulness. "Royal" imparts a fine appearance, and a particularly good flavor to the food.

Housekeepers are urged to avoid substitutes for Royal Baking Powder. Failures in baking often result from the use of sour milk and soda, or even home made mixtures of cream of tartar and soda, because of inability to determine the uncertain strength of such materials and hence the proper proportions to use.

Avoid all guess work by using "Royal." It is always the same, always dependable.

SOME SECRETS OF GOOD COOKING

The addition of one or two teaspoons of Royal Baking Powder to plain pastry will add wonderfully to its qualities, making it very light and tender.

Omelets are improved by the addition of a small amount of Royal Baking Powder.

Royal Baking Powder may be added with great advantage to *bread pudding, poultry dressing, stuffed* or *deviled crabs* and other preparations in which broken bread or bread crumbs are used.

Icings and especially Ornamental Icings are improved in texture and flavor by the addition of about a teaspoon of Royal Baking Powder.

Instead of adding soda to keep color in green vegetables use Royal Baking Powder.

ROYAL BAKING POWDER

For raising or leavening breads, biscuits, rolls, muffins, griddle cakes, doughnuts, cakes, pastries, puddings and other similar foods.

ABSOLUTELY PURE AND WHOLESOME

The principal active ingredient of Royal Baking Powder is Royal Grape Cream of Tartar, a derivative of rich, ripe grapes. It perfectly aerates and leavens the batter or dough and makes the food finer in appearance, more delicious to the taste, and more healthful.

It possesses the greatest practicable leavening strength, never varies in quality, and will keep fresh and perfect in all climates until used.

THE STANDARD FOR OVER 50 YEARS

For over 50 years Royal Baking Powder has been the standard. Most of the famous baking recipes in use today were created with it. Most of the famous cooking schools use it. Housewives all over the world have followed the lead of the American housewife and insist upon it. "I must have La Royal," say our Spanish-speaking neighbors in Mexico, Cuba and South America. "I want Royal Baking Powder and no other," say housewives in England, Scotland and Ireland.

Only unequalled quality could create such a world-wide demand.

USED IN LEADING HOTELS

Prominent chefs and expert bakers in America, including those of the famous restaurants in New York, Chicago, San Francisco and other cities, consider Royal Baking Powder the most reliable, most efficient and the most dependable leavening agent.

Physicians recommend Royal Baking Powder for its wholesomeness and for the healthful qualities that it adds to the food.

For Making the Finest and Most Healthful Food, Royal Baking Powder is Indispensable.

GENERAL SUGGESTIONS

Where shortening is mentioned in the recipes it is understood that butter or lard, or an equivalent quantity of butter substitute or vegetable oil may be used.

MEASUREMENTS

All measurements for all materials called for in the recipes in this book are level.

The standard measuring cup holds one-half pint and is divided into fourths and thirds.

To make level measurements fill cup or spoon and scrape off excess with back of knife.

One-half spoon is measured lengthwise of spoon.

Sift flour before measuring.

BAKING

Regulate the oven carefully before mixing the ingredients. Many a cake otherwise perfectly prepared is spoiled because the oven is too hot or not hot enough.

Biscuits and pastry require a hot oven; cakes, a moderate oven.

When a cake is thoroughly baked it shrinks from the sides of the pan. A light touch with the finger which leaves no mark is another indication that the cake is baked.

TABLE OF EQUIVALENT WEIGHTS AND MEASURES

1 saltspoon	= 1/4 teaspoon
3 teaspoons	= 1 tablespoon
16 tablespoons	= 1 cup
2 cups	= 1 pint
2 pints	= 1 quart
4 cups	= 1 quart
2 cups granulated sugar	= 1 pound
4 cups flour	= 1 pound
2 cups butter	= 1 pound

2 tablespoons butter = 1 ounce

2 tablespoons liquid = 1 ounce

4 tablespoons flour = 1 ounce

1 square unsweetened chocolate = 1 ounce

All measurements are level. Four level teaspoons of baking powder about equal one heaping teaspoon as heretofore used.

[Note: The following 6 lines are notes at the top of pages which are repeated throughout the original book.]

Royal Baking Powder Contains No Alum

Royal Baking Powder Is Absolutely Pure

Royal Baking Powder Leaves No Bitter Taste

Royal is Made from Cream of Tartar

Royal Baking Powder Never Disturbs Digestion

Bake it with Royal and be Sure

CONTENTS

BREAD AND ROLLS

Royal Baking Powder may be used instead of yeast to leaven bread. It does the same work; that is, raises the dough, making it porous and spongy.

The great advantage in baking powder bread is in time saved. Royal Baking Powder bread can be mixed and baked in about an hour and a half.

ROYAL BAKING POWDER BREAD

4 cups flour
1 teaspoon salt
1 tablespoon sugar
7 teaspoons Royal Baking Powder
1 medium-sized, cold boiled potato
milk (water may be used)

Sift together flour, salt, sugar and baking powder, rub in potato; add sufficient milk to mix smoothly into stiff batter. Turn at once into greased loaf pan, smooth top with knife dipped in melted butter, and allow to stand in warm place about 30 minutes. Bake in moderate oven about one hour. When done take from pan, moisten top with few drops cold water and allow to cool before putting away in bread box.

BOSTON BROWN BREAD

1 cup entire wheat or graham flour
1 cup corn meal
1 cup rye meal or ground rolled oats
5 teaspoons Royal Baking Powder
1 teaspoon salt
3/4 cup molasses
1-1/3 cups milk

Mix thoroughly dry ingredients; add molasses to milk, and add to dry ingredients; beat thoroughly and put into greased moulds 2/3 full. Steam 3-1/2 hours; remove covers and bake until top is dry.

SPIDER CORN BREAD

1 egg
1-3/4 cups milk
1 cup corn meal

1/3 cup flour
2 tablespoons sugar
1 teaspoon salt
2 teaspoons Royal Baking Powder
1 tablespoon shortening

Beat egg and add one cup milk; stir in corn meal, flour, sugar, salt and baking powder which have been sifted together; turn into frying pan in which shortening has been melted; pour on remainder of milk but do not stir. Bake about 25 minutes in hot oven. There should be a line of creamy custard through the bread. Cut into triangles and serve.

CORN BREAD

1 cup corn meal
1 cup flour
4 teaspoons Royal Baking Powder
3 tablespoons sugar
1 teaspoon salt
1-1/2 cups milk
2 tablespoons melted shortening
1 egg

Mix and sift dry ingredients; add milk, shortening and beaten egg; beat well and pour into greased shallow pan. Bake in hot oven about 25 minutes.

CORN AND RICE PONE

2 cups corn meal
5 teaspoons Royal Baking Powder
1 teaspoon salt
3 eggs
2-1/4 cups milk
4 tablespoons melted shortening
1 cup boiled rice

Mix and sift dry ingredients; add milk and shortening to beaten eggs; stir into dry mixture; mix in rice and pour into shallow greased pans. Bake in hot oven about 30 minutes.

GRAHAM BREAD

1-1/2 cups flour
1-1/2 cups graham flour
4 teaspoons Royal Baking Powder
1 teaspoon salt
1 tablespoon melted shortening
1 egg
1-1/2 cups liquid (1/2 water and 1/2 milk)
2 tablespoons sugar or molasses

Mix flour, graham flour, baking powder and salt together; add beaten egg, shortening and sugar or molasses to liquid; stir into dry mixture and beat well; add more milk if necessary to make a drop batter. Put into greased loaf pan, smooth with knife dipped in cold water. Bake about one hour in moderate oven.

NUT AND RAISIN BREAD

1-1/2 cups flour
2 cups graham flour
1/2 cup corn meal
1/2 cup brown sugar
1 teaspoon salt
4 teaspoons Royal Baking Powder
3/4 cup chopped nuts
1 cup ground raisins
2 cups milk
1/2 cup molasses
1/4 teaspoon soda

Sift dry ingredients together. Add nuts and raisins; add milk and mix well, then add molasses and soda which have been mixed together. Bake in two small greased loaf pans in moderate oven about 45 minutes.

PEANUT BUTTER BREAD

2 cups flour
4 teaspoons Royal Baking Powder
1 teaspoon salt
1/2 cup sugar
2/3 cup peanut butter
1 cup milk

Sift flour, baking powder, salt and sugar together. Add milk to peanut butter, blend well and add to dry ingredients; beat thoroughly. Bake in greased loaf pan in slow oven 45 to 50 minutes. This is best when a day old. It makes delicious sandwiches cut in thin slices and filled with either cream cheese or lettuce and mayonnaise.

PRUNE OR DATE BREAD

1 cup prunes or dates
2-1/2 cups graham flour or 1 cup flour and 1-1/2 cups graham flour
1/4 cup sugar
1 teaspoon salt
4 teaspoons Royal Baking Powder
1 cup milk
1 tablespoon melted shortening

Stone and chop fruit (prunes must be soaked several hours and drained). Mix flour, sugar, salt and baking powder; add milk and beat well; add fruit and shortening. Put into greased bread pan; allow to stand 20 to 25 minutes in warm place. Bake in moderate oven one hour.

LUNCHEON OR SANDWICH ROLLS

4 cups flour
1 teaspoon salt
6 teaspoons Royal Baking Powder
1 tablespoon shortening
1-1/2 cups milk

Sift together flour, salt and baking powder; rub in shortening; add milk, and mix with spoon to smooth dough easy to handle on floured board. Turn out dough; knead quickly a few times to impart smoothness; divide into small pieces; form each by hand into short, rather thick tapering rolls; place on greased pans and allow to stand in warm place 15 to 20 minutes; brush with milk. Bake in very hot oven. When almost baked brush again with melted butter. Bake 10 minutes longer and serve hot. If a glazed finish is desired, before taking from oven brush with yolk of egg which has been mixed with a little water. These rolls make excellent sandwiches, using for fillings either lettuce and mayonnaise, sliced or chopped ham, chopped seasoned cucumbers, egg and mayonnaise with very little chopped onion and parsley, or other filling desired.

RYE ROLLS

4 cups rye flour
1 teaspoon salt
6 teaspoons Royal Baking Powder
1-1/2 cups milk
1 tablespoon shortening

Sift together dry ingredients; add milk and melted shortening. Knead on floured board; shape into rolls. Put into greased pans and allow to stand in warm place 20 minutes. Bake in moderate oven 25 to 30 minutes.

POTATO ROLLS

4 cups flour
1 teaspoon salt
1 tablespoon sugar
7 teaspoons Royal Baking Powder
2 medium-sized cold, boiled potatoes
water or milk

Sift thoroughly together flour, salt, sugar and baking powder; rub in potatoes or add after putting through ricer; add sufficient liquid to mix smoothly into soft dough. This will require about one and one-half cups. Divide into small pieces; knead each and shape into small rolls; place on greased pan and brush with melted shortening and allow to stand in warm place 15 to 20 minutes. Bake in hot oven and when nearly done, brush again with melted shortening.

NUT AND RAISIN ROLLS

2-1/2 cups flour
4 teaspoons Royal Baking Powder
1/2 teaspoon salt
1 tablespoon sugar
5 tablespoons shortening
1 egg
2/3 cup milk
butter
raisins
chopped nuts
1/2 cup sugar

Sift flour, baking powder, salt and sugar together. Add melted shortening and beaten egg to milk and add to dry ingredients, mixing well. Turn out on floured board and knead lightly. Roll out very thin. Spread with butter and sprinkle with raisins, chopped nuts and small amount of granulated sugar. Cut into about 4-inch squares. Roll up each as for jelly roll. Press edges together. Brush over with yolk of egg mixed with a little cold water and sprinkle with nuts and sugar, and allow to stand in greased pan about 15 minutes. Bake in moderate oven from 20 to 25 minutes.

PARKER HOUSE ROLLS

4 cups flour
1 teaspoon salt
6 teaspoons Royal Baking Powder
2-4 tablespoons shortening
1-1/2 cups milk

Sift flour, salt and baking powder together. Add melted shortening to milk and add slowly to dry ingredients stirring until smooth. Knead on floured board and roll one-half inch thick. Cut with biscuit cutter. Crease each circle with back of knife one side of center. Butter small section and fold larger part well over small. Place one inch apart in greased pan. Allow to stand 15 minutes in warm place. Brush with melted butter and bake in hot oven 15 to 20 minutes.

RUSKS

2-1/4 cups flour
1/2 teaspoon salt
2 tablespoons maple or brown sugar
4 teaspoons Royal Baking Powder
1/4 teaspoon nutmeg
3/4 teaspoon cinnamon
1 egg
1/3 to 2/3 cup water
2 tablespoons shortening

Sift together flour, salt, sugar, baking powder, nutmeg and cinnamon; add beaten egg and melted shortening to water and add. Mix well and turn out on floured board. Divide into small pieces; with floured hands shape into rolls; place on greased shallow pan close together; allow to stand 10 to 15 minutes before baking; brush with milk and sprinkle with a little maple or brown sugar. Bake in moderate oven 20 to 30 minutes.

For hot cross buns, with sharp knife make deep cross cuts; brush with butter, sprinkle with sugar and bake.

ROYAL CINNAMON BUNS

2-1/4 cups flour
1 teaspoon salt
4 teaspoons Royal Baking Powder
2 tablespoons shortening
1 egg
1/2 cup water
1/2 cup sugar
2 teaspoons cinnamon
4 tablespoons seeded raisins

Sift 2 tablespoons of measured sugar with flour, salt and baking powder; rub shortening in lightly; add beaten egg to water and add slowly. Roll out 1/4-inch thick on floured board; brush with melted butter, sprinkle with sugar, cinnamon and raisins. Roll as for jelly roll; cut into 1-1/2-inch pieces; place with cut edges up on greased pan; sprinkle with sugar and cinnamon. Bake in moderate oven 30 to 35 minutes; remove from pan at once.

BROWN SUGAR BUNS

2 cups flour
4 teaspoons Royal Baking Powder
1/2 teaspoon salt
1 tablespoon shortening
1/2 cup milk
1 tablespoon butter
1 cup brown sugar

Sift together flour, baking powder and salt; add shortening and rub in very lightly; add milk slowly to make a soft dough; roll out 1/4-inch thick. Have butter soft and spread over dough; cover with brown sugar. Roll same as jelly roll; cut into 1-1/2-inch pieces and place with cut edges up on well greased pan. Bake in moderate oven about 30 minutes; remove from pan at once.

COFFEE CAKE

2 cups flour
1/2 teaspoon salt
3 tablespoons sugar

4 teaspoons Royal Baking Powder
2 tablespoons shortening
2/3 cup milk

Mix and sift dry ingredients; add melted shortening and enough milk to make very stiff batter. Spread 1/2-inch thick in greased pan; add top mixture. Bake about 30 minutes in moderate oven.

TOP MIXTURE

2 tablespoons flour
1 tablespoon cinnamon
3 tablespoons sugar
3 tablespoons shortening

Mix dry ingredients; rub in shortening and spread thickly over top of dough before baking.

ROYAL INDIVIDUAL COFFEE CAKES

2 cups flour
3/4 teaspoon salt
4 tablespoons sugar
3 teaspoons Royal Baking Powder
4 tablespoons shortening
1 egg
1/2 cup milk

Sift dry ingredients together; mix in shortening; add beaten egg to milk and add to dry ingredients to make soft dough; divide dough into six long, narrow pieces; with hands roll out on board each piece very long and thin; spread with butter; cut each in two and beginning in center twist two pieces together and bring ends around to form crescent. Put into greased pan; sprinkle with chopped nuts. Bake in hot oven 15 to 20 minutes. While hot, brush over with thin icing made with 1/2 cup confectioner's sugar moistened with 1 tablespoon hot water.

RAISIN TEA RING

3 cups flour
6 tablespoons sugar
4 teaspoons Royal Baking Powder
1 teaspoon salt
1/2 to 3/4 cup milk
3 tablespoons shortening
1 egg
1 cup raisins, washed, drained and floured
1/2 cup chopped nuts

Sift dry ingredients together; add raisins; to milk add melted shortening and beaten egg, and add to dry ingredients to make a soft dough; roll out lightly about

1/2-inch thick; divide into two long strips and twist together to form a ring; put into greased pan and sprinkle with sugar and nuts; allow to stand about 20 minutes. Bake in moderate oven 20 to 25 minutes.

BISCUITS AND MUFFINS

Of all foods for breakfast, nothing is so appetizing and satisfying, as light, flaky, hot Royal Baking Powder Biscuit, with a crisp, brown crust, just from the oven, broken apart and spread with butter, honey, jam or marmalade.

BISCUITS

2 cups flour
4 teaspoons Royal Baking Powder
1/2 teaspoon salt
2 tablespoons shortening
3/4 cup milk or half milk and half water

Sift together flour, baking powder and salt, add shortening and rub in very lightly; add liquid slowly; roll or pat on floured board to about one inch in thickness (handle as little as possible); cut with biscuit cutter. Bake in hot oven 15 to 20 minutes.

EMERGENCY OR DROP BISCUITS

Same as recipe for biscuits with the addition of more milk to make stiff batter. Drop by spoonfuls on greased pan and bake in hot oven.

WHOLE WHEAT OR HEALTH BISCUITS

2 cups whole wheat flour
3/4 teaspoon salt
4 teaspoons Royal Baking Powder
2 teaspoons shortening
1 cup milk
4 tablespoons cut raisins

Mix well flour, salt and baking powder, or sift through coarse strainer; rub shortening in lightly; add milk; mix to soft dough, add raisins. Drop with tablespoon quite far apart on greased baking tin or in muffin tins. Bake in moderate oven about 25 minutes.

BRAN BISCUITS

1/2 cup bran
1-1/2 cups flour
5 teaspoons Royal Baking Powder

3/4 teaspoon salt
3 tablespoons sugar
1/2 cup water
2 tablespoons melted shortening

Mix thoroughly bran, flour, baking powder, salt, sugar; add sufficient water to make soft dough; add shortening; roll on floured board to about 1/4-inch thick; cut with biscuit cutter. Bake in hot oven 12 to 15 minutes.

CHEESE BISCUITS

1-1/2 cups flour
2 teaspoons Royal Baking Powder
1/4 teaspoon salt
1 teaspoon shortening
6 tablespoons grated cheese
5/8 cup milk

Sift together flour, baking powder and salt; add shortening and cheese; mix in lightly; add milk slowly, just enough to hold dough together. Roll out on floured board about 1/2-inch thick; cut with biscuit cutter. Bake in hot oven 12 to 15 minutes.

TEA BISCUITS

2 cups flour
3 teaspoons Royal Baking Powder
1/2 teaspoon salt
1 tablespoon sugar
1 egg
2 tablespoons shortening
1/3 cup water

Sift together flour, baking powder, salt and sugar; add well-beaten egg and melted shortening to water and add to dry ingredients to make soft dough. Roll out on floured board to about 1/2-inch thick; cut with biscuit cutter. Bake in moderate oven about 25 minutes.

MUFFINS

2 cups flour
3 teaspoons Royal Baking Powder
1 tablespoon sugar
1/2 teaspoon salt
1 cup milk
2 eggs
1 tablespoon shortening

Sift together flour, baking powder, sugar and salt; add milk, well-beaten eggs and melted shortening; mix well. Half fill greased muffin tins and bake in hot oven

20 to 25 minutes.

BLUEBERRY OR HUCKLEBERRY MUFFINS

2 cups flour
3 teaspoons Royal Baking Powder
1 teaspoon salt
1 tablespoon sugar
3/4 cup milk
2 eggs
1 tablespoon shortening
1 cup berries

Sift together flour, baking powder, salt and sugar; add milk slowly, well-beaten eggs and melted shortening; mix well and add berries, which have been carefully picked over and floured. Grease muffin tins; drop one spoonful into each. Bake about 30 minutes in moderate oven.

CEREAL MUFFINS

1/2 cup cooked hominy, oatmeal or other cereal
1/2 teaspoon salt
1-1/2 tablespoons shortening
1 egg
1/2 cup milk
1 cup flour
1/2 cup corn meal
4 teaspoons Royal Baking Powder

Mix together cereal, salt, melted shortening, beaten egg and milk. Add flour and corn meal which have been sifted with baking powder; beat well. Bake in greased muffin tins or shallow pan in hot oven 25 to 30 minutes.

CORN MEAL MUFFINS

3/4 cup corn meal
1-1/4 cups flour
4 teaspoons Royal Baking Powder
1/2 teaspoon salt
2 tablespoons sugar
1 cup milk
2 tablespoons shortening
1 egg

Sift together corn meal, flour, baking powder, salt and sugar; add milk, melted shortening and well-beaten egg; mix well. Half fill greased muffin tins and bake about 35 minutes in hot oven.

CRUMB MUFFINS

    2 cups stale bread crumbs
    1-1/4 cups milk
    1 cup flour
    2 teaspoons Royal Baking Powder
    1/2 teaspoon salt
    2 eggs
    1 tablespoon shortening

Soak bread crumbs in cold milk 10 minutes; add flour, baking powder and salt which have been sifted together; add well-beaten eggs and melted shortening; mix well. Heat muffin tins, grease and drop one tablespoon of batter into each. Bake 20 to 25 minutes in hot oven.

RICE MUFFINS

    1 cup flour
    2 teaspoons Royal Baking Powder
    1/2 teaspoon salt
    1 tablespoon sugar
    2/3 cup milk
    1 egg
    1 tablespoon shortening
    1 cup cold boiled rice

Sift together flour, baking powder, salt and sugar; add milk slowly; then well-beaten egg and melted shortening; add rice and mix well. Grease muffin tins; drop one spoonful of mixture into each. Bake 20 to 30 minutes in hot oven.

DATE MUFFINS

    1/3 cup butter
    1 egg
    2 cups flour
    2 teaspoons Royal Baking Powder
    1/2 teaspoon salt
    3/4 cup milk
    1/2 pound dates

Cream butter, add beaten egg, flour in which baking powder and salt have been sifted, and milk. Stir in dates which have been pitted and cut into small pieces. Bake about 25 minutes in greased gem pans in hot oven.

For sweet muffins sift 1/4 cup sugar with dry ingredients.

SCONES

    2 cups flour
    3 teaspoons Royal Baking Powder
    1 teaspoon salt
    2 tablespoons sugar

2 tablespoons shortening
2 eggs
1/3 cup milk

Sift together flour, baking powder, salt and sugar; add shortening and mix in very lightly. Beat eggs until light; add milk to eggs and add slowly to mixture. Roll out 1/2-inch thick on floured board; cut into pieces 3 inches square and fold over, making them three-cornered; brush with milk; dust with sugar. Bake about 25 minutes in hot oven.

CURRANT TEA CAKES

2 cups flour
3 teaspoons Royal Baking Powder
1/2 cup sugar
3/4 teaspoon salt
1 cup milk
1 egg
2 tablespoons shortening
1/2 cup currants

Sift together flour, baking powder, sugar and salt; add beaten egg and melted shortening to milk and add to dry ingredients; add currants which have been washed, dried and floured; mix well. The batter should be stiff. Grease hot muffin tins and fill half full. Bake about 20 minutes in hot oven.

POPOVERS

2 cups flour
1/2 teaspoon salt
2 eggs
2 cups milk

Sift together flour and salt. Make a well in flour, break eggs into well, add milk and stir until smooth. Pour into hot greased gem pans and bake 25 to 35 minutes in very hot oven. If taken out of oven too soon they will fall.

GRAHAM GEMS

1 cup graham flour
1 cup flour
3/4 teaspoon salt
4 teaspoons Royal Baking Powder
1 cup milk
1 egg
2 tablespoons molasses or sugar
3 tablespoons shortening

Mix together dry ingredients; add milk, beaten egg, molasses and melted shortening. Bake in greased gem pans in hot oven about 25 minutes.

GREEN CORN GEMS

2 cups green corn put through food chopper
1/4 cup milk, or 1/2 cup if corn is dry
2 eggs
2 cups flour
3 teaspoons Royal Baking Powder
1 teaspoon salt
1/8 teaspoon pepper

To the corn add milk and well-beaten eggs; add flour, baking powder, salt and pepper which have been sifted together; mix well. Drop into hot greased gem pans. Bake in hot oven 20 to 25 minutes.

FIG ENVELOPES

2 cups flour
3 teaspoons Royal Baking Powder
1/2 teaspoon salt
2 tablespoons sugar
2 teaspoons shortening
2/3 cup milk
1 cup chopped figs
1 egg

Sift together flour, baking powder, salt and sugar; add shortening and mix in very lightly; add slowly enough milk to form soft dough. Dust board with flour and roll out dough 1/4-inch thick, cut into squares and on each piece put one tablespoon of fig; brush edges with cold milk; fold like an envelope, and press edges together. Brush tops with egg beaten with one tablespoon milk and one teaspoon sugar. Bake about 20 minutes in hot oven.

SALLY LUNN

2 cups flour
3 teaspoons Royal Baking Powder
1 teaspoon salt
1 tablespoon sugar
3/4 cup milk
2 eggs
2 tablespoons shortening

Sift together flour, baking powder, salt and sugar; add milk, well-beaten eggs and melted shortening; mix well. Bake in greased shallow pan or muffin tins in moderate oven about 25 minutes.

GRIDDLE CAKES AND WAFFLES

Griddle cakes, as made today with Royal Baking Powder have become most popular. Properly made they are delicious, healthful, appetizing and nutritious.

The batter must be thin. The cakes should be small and not top thick—about one-eighth inch when baked.

An iron frying pan may be used instead of griddle. In any case grease only enough to keep the cakes from sticking. Turn only once.

ROYAL HOT GRIDDLE CAKES

2 cups flour
1/2 teaspoon salt
5 teaspoons Royal Baking Powder
1-1/2 cups milk
2 tablespoons shortening

Mix and sift dry ingredients; add milk and melted shortening; beat well. Bake on slightly greased hot griddle.

GRIDDLE CAKES WITH EGGS

1-3/4 cups flour
1/2 teaspoon salt
3 teaspoons Royal Baing Powder
1-1/2 cups milk
1 tablespoon shortening

Mix and sift dry ingredients; add beaten eggs, milk and melted shortening; mix well. Bake on slightly greased hot griddle turning only once.

BUCKWHEAT CAKES

2 cups buckwheat flour
1 cup flour
6 teaspoons Royal Baking Powder
1-1/2 teaspoons salt
2-1/2 cups milk or milk and water
1 tablespoon molasses
1 tablespoon melted shortening

Sift together flours, baking powder and salt; add molasses and shortening to liquid; beat well. Bake on hot slightly greased griddle turning only once.

CORN MEAL GRIDDLE CAKES

1-1/3 cups corn meal
1-1/2 cups boiling water
1 tablespoon shortening
3/4 cup milk
1 tablespoon molasses
2/3 cup flour
1 teaspoon salt
4 teaspoons Royal Baking Powder

Scald corn meal with boiling water; add shortening, milk and molasses; add flour, salt and baking powder which have been sifted together; mix well. Bake on hot, slightly greased griddle turning once.

RICE GRIDDLE CAKES

1 cup boiled rice
1 cup milk
1 tablespoon shortening
1 teaspoon salt
1 egg
1 cup flour
2 teaspoons Royal Baking Powder

Mix rice, milk, melted shortening, salt and well-beaten egg; stir in flour and baking powder which have been sifted together; mix well. Bake on hot, slightly greased griddle turning only once.

FRENCH PANCAKES

1 cup flour
2 teaspoons Royal Baking Powder
1/2 teaspoon salt
2 eggs
1 tablespoon sugar
2 cups milk
1/2 cup cream
jam
powdered sugar

Sift together flour, baking powder and salt. Add eggs which have been beaten with the sugar, milk, and cream. Batter should be very thin. Heat small frying pan in which a little butter has been melted. Pour in just sufficient batter to cover bottom of pan. Cook over hot fire. Turn and brown other side. Spread with jam and roll up. Sprinkle with powdered sugar and serve hot.

WHOLE WHEAT HOT CAKES

2 cups whole wheat flour
4 teaspoons Royal Baking Powder
1/2 teaspoon salt
1-3/4 cups milk
1 teaspoon molasses
1 tablespoon melted shortening
2 eggs

Sift together flour, baking powder and salt; add milk, molasses, and shortening to beaten eggs and add to dry ingredients; mix well. Bake on hot, slightly greased griddle turning only once.

WAFFLES

2 cups flour
4 teaspoons Royal Baking Powder
3/4 teaspoon salt
1-3/4 cups milk
2 eggs
1 tablespoon melted shortening

Sift flour, baking powder and salt together; add milk and shortening to egg yolks, and add to dry ingredients; mix in beaten egg whites. Bake in well greased hot waffle iron until brown; turn once. Serve hot with butter and maple syrup.

FRITTERS

Fritters are served for luncheon, dinner or supper, as an entree, a vegetable or a sweet, according to the ingredients used. The foundation batter is much the same for all fritters, and with some additions the first recipe given can be used for many varieties. By the use of Royal Baking Powder, a fine fritter batter may be stirred up in a few minutes.

Fritters should be fried in deep fat, hot enough to brown a piece of bread in 60 seconds.

PLAIN FRITTER BATTER

1 cup flour
1-1/2 teaspoons Royal Baking Powder
1/4 teaspoon salt
1 egg
2/3 cup milk

Sift dry ingredients together; add beaten egg and milk; beat until smooth.

APPLE FRITTERS

4 large apples
2 tablespoons powdered sugar
1 tablespoon lemon juice

Peel and core apples and cut into slices; add sugar and lemon juice. Dip each slice into plain fritter batter. Fry light brown in deep fat. Drain and sprinkle with powdered sugar.

FRUIT FRITTERS

Fruits other than apples may be used in fritters by following the directions for apple fritters. Canned whole fruits drained from syrup may also, be used. Chop fruit (not too fine) and stir into plain fritter batter. Drop by spoonfuls into deep hot fat, turning until brown. Drain and sprinkle with powdered sugar.

BANANA FRITTERS

1 cup flour
2 teaspoons Royal Baking Powder
1 tablespoon powdered sugar

1/4 teaspoon salt
1 egg
1/4 cup milk
1 tablespoon lemon juice
3 bananas

Mix and sift dry ingredients. Add others in order. Force bananas through sieve before adding. Beat thoroughly. Drop by spoonfuls into hot fat. Drain and sprinkle with powdered sugar.

CORN FRITTERS

1/2 cup milk
2 cups cooked corn
1-1/2 cups flour
1 teaspoon salt
1/3 teaspoon pepper
2 teaspoons Royal Baking Powder
1 tablespoon melted shortening
2 eggs

Add milk to corn; add flour sifted with salt, pepper and baking powder; add shortening and beaten eggs; beat well. Fry by spoonfuls on hot greased griddle or frying pan.

If fried in deep fat make batter stiffer by adding 1/2 cup flour and 1 teaspoon Royal Baking Powder.

CLAM FRITTERS

1-1/2 cups flour
2 teaspoons Royal Baking Powder
1/2 teaspoon salt
1/3 teaspoon pepper
1/3 teaspoon paprika
1/2 cup milk or clam juice
2 eggs
1-1/2 teaspoons grated onion
1 teaspoon melted shortening
10 clams

Sift together dry ingredients; add liquid, beaten eggs, onion, and shortening; rinse clams, put through meat chopper and add to batter. Take one spoonful batter for each fritter and fry on hot greased griddle or in deep fat.

CAKE

In no department of cookery is Royal Baking Powder of more use and importance than in making fine cake.

Where fewer eggs are used, increase the amount of Royal Baking Powder about one teaspoon for each egg omitted.

If an unsalted shortening is used take slightly less and add a small quantity of salt.

Sift flour before measuring.

The baking of cake is of primary importance. Regulate the oven before putting materials together. See general suggestions, page 2.

PLAIN CAKE

1/4 cup shortening
1 cup sugar
1 egg
1 teaspoon vanilla extract
1 cup milk
2 cups flour
3 teaspoons Royal Baking Powder
1/2 teaspoon salt

Cream shortening; add sugar slowly, add well beaten egg and flavoring; sift together flour, baking powder and salt and add to mixture a little at a time, alternately with milk. Bake in greased loaf, layer or patty pans in moderate oven. May also be used hot for cottage pudding.

SUNSHINE CAKE

3 tablespoons shortening
3/4 cup sugar
yolks of 3 eggs
1 teaspoon flavoring extract
1-1/2 cups flour
3 teaspoons Royal Baking Powder
1/2 cup milk

Cream shortening; add sugar gradually, and yolks of eggs which have been beaten until thick; add flavoring; sift together flour and baking powder and add alternately, a little at a time, with the milk to first mixture. Bake in greased loaf pan in moderate oven 35 to 45 minutes. Cover with white icing, page 16.

Note—This is an excellent cake to make in combination with the following Three-Egg Angel Cake. Only three eggs are required for both.

THREE-EGG ANGEL CAKE

1 cup sugar.
1-1/3 cups flour
1/2 teaspoon cream of tartar
3 teaspoons Royal Baking Powder
1/3 teaspoon salt
2/3 cup scalded milk
1 teaspoon almond or vanilla extract
whites of 3 eggs

METHOD I

Mix and sift first five ingredients four times. Add milk very slowly, while still hot, beating continually; add vanilla; mix well and fold in whites of eggs beaten until light. Turn into ungreased angel cake tin and bake in very slow oven about 45 minutes. Remove from oven; invert pan and allow to stand until cold. Cover with white or chocolate icing, **page 16**.

METHOD II

Boil sugar with cold milk until thick and pour very slowly over whites of eggs which have been beaten light with a wire whip. Fold in flour, cream of tartar, salt and baking powder which have been sifted together five times. With whip beat mixture with long strokes until very light; add flavoring; put into ungreased angel cake tin in cold oven, turn on heat and bake at very low temperature for 25 minutes. Raise temperature slightly and bake 30 minutes longer or until thoroughly baked. Remove from oven, invert pan and allow to stand until cold. Cover with white or chocolate icing, **page 16**.

ANGEL CAKE

whites of 8 eggs
1 teaspoon cream of tartar
3/4 cup granulated sugar
1/4 teaspoon salt
1 teaspoon Royal Baking Powder
3/4 cup flour
1 teaspoon vanilla extract

Whip whites of eggs to firm, stiff froth; add cream of tartar; fold sugar in lightly; fold in flour which has been sifted four times with baking powder and salt; add vanilla. Pour into ungreased pan and bake 45 to 50 minutes in moderate oven. Remove from oven; invert pan and allow to stand until cold. Ice with either chocolate or white icing, page 16.

SPANISH CAKE

1/2 cup shortening
1 cup sugar
2 eggs
1-3/4 cups flour
3 teaspoons Royal Baking Powder
1 teaspoon cinnamon
1/2 cup milk

Cream shortening; add sugar and yolks of eggs; beat well; sift together flour, baking powder and cinnamon and add alternately with milk; fold in beaten whites of eggs. Bake in greased pan in moderate oven 35 to 40 minutes. Cover with boiled icing, page 16.

BRIDE'S CAKE

1 cup shortening
2 cups sugar
1 teaspoon almond or vanilla extract
3/4 cup milk
3-1/2 cups flour
3 teaspoons Royal Baking Powder
whites of six eggs

Beat shortening to a cream, adding sugar gradually; add flavoring extract; beat until smooth. Add alternately a little at a time milk and flour which has been sifted three times with baking powder. Beat whites of eggs until dry, and add to batter, folding in very lightly without beating. Bake in greased loaf pan in moderate oven about one hour.

EGGLESS, MILKLESS, BUTTERLESS CAKE

1 cup brown sugar
1-1/4 cups water
1 cup seeded raisins
2 ounces citron, cut fine
1/3 cup shortening
1/2 teaspoon salt
1 teaspoon nutmeg
1 teaspoon cinnamon
2 cups flour
5 teaspoons Royal Baking Powder

Boil sugar, water, fruit, shortening, salt and spices together in saucepan 3 minutes; when cool, add flour and baking powder which have been sifted together; mix well. Bake in greased loaf pan in moderate oven about 45 minutes.

CHOCOLATE CAKE

3 squares unsweetened chocolate
2 tablespoons sugar
1-1/2 tablespoons milk
4 tablespoons shortening
1 cup sugar
2 eggs
2/3 cup milk
1-1/3 cups flour
2 teaspoons Royal Baking Powder
1/8 teaspoon salt

Cook slowly until smooth first three ingredients. Cream shortening; add sugar and beat well. Add yolks of eggs and beat again. Stir in chocolate mixture and then add alternately the milk and flour which has been sifted with the baking powder and salt. Fold in the beaten whites of eggs. Bake in greased loaf pan in moderate oven 50 to 60 minutes. Cover with white or chocolate icing, page 16.

POUND CAKE

1 cup butter
1 cup sugar
1 teaspoon vanilla extract
1 teaspoon lemon extract
5 eggs
2 cups flour
1 teaspoon Royal Baking Powder
Reserve 2 egg whites for icing

Cream butter, add sugar slowly, beating well. Add flavoring and yolks of eggs which have been beaten until pale yellow. Beat three egg whites until light and add alternately a little at a time with the flour which has been sifted with baking powder. Mix well and bake in greased loaf pan in moderate oven about one hour. Cover with ornamental frosting, page 16, made with the two remaining egg whites.

RICH FRUIT CAKE

2 cups shortening
2 cups sugar
6 eggs
4 cups seeded raisins
4 cups currants
4 cups flour
1 cup shelled almonds
2 tablespoons orange peel
2 tablespoons lemon peel
2 cups sliced citron

1 cup grape juice
2 teaspoons cinnamon
1/2 teaspoon grated nutmeg
1/2 teaspoon ground mace
1/4 teaspoon allspice
1/2 teaspoon cloves
1/2 teaspoon salt
4 teaspoons Royal Baking Powder

Cream shortening and sugar together; add beaten egg yolks; add raisins and currants, which have been washed, dried, and over which a cup and a half of the flour has been sifted; blanch almonds and put through food chopper with lemon and orange peel and add; slice citron very fine and add; stir in grape juice and half of stiffly beaten whites of eggs; sift together spices, salt, baking powder and flour and add; mix well and fold in remaining whites; pour into two 12-inch pans which have been lined with four layers of brown paper and bake in moderate oven one hour; then cover with double layer of brown paper; put asbestos plates underneath and continue baking about two hours longer.

COFFEE FRUIT CAKE

1/2 cup shortening
1 cup light brown sugar
2 eggs
1/4 cup strong coffee
1/3 cup rich milk or cream
1-3/4 cups flour
3 teaspoons Royal Baking Powder
1/2 lb. raisins
1/8 lb. sliced citron
1/4 lb. figs, cut in strips

Cream shortening; add sugar; add egg yolks, coffee and milk; sift together flour and baking powder and add slowly; add fruit, which has been slightly floured, and fold in beaten whites of eggs. Bake in greased loaf pan from 60 to 90 minutes.

ROYAL DATE CAKE

1 cup boiling water
1 lb. stoned and cut dates
3/4 cup brown sugar
2 tablespoons shortening
1 square melted chocolate
1 egg
2 teaspoons Royal Baking Powder
1/4 teaspoon salt
1-3/4 cups flour

3/4 cup chopped pecan nuts

Pour boiling water over dates. Cream sugar and shortening; add chocolate and beaten egg; mix well and add dates and water; sift baking powder, salt and flour together; add gradually with pecan nuts. Bake in greased loaf pan in slow oven one and a half hours.

ROYAL CREAM LOAF CAKE

1/2 cup shortening
1 cup sugar
2 eggs
1 teaspoon lemon extract
1/2 cup rich milk or thin cream
1 cup flour
1/2 cup corn starch
3 teaspoons Royal Baking Powder

Cream shortening; add sugar slowly; add beaten yolks of eggs and flavoring; add milk a little at a time; sift flour, corn starch and baking powder together and add; fold in beaten whites of eggs. Bake in greased loaf pan in moderate oven 35 to 45 minutes, and cover with frosting, page 16.

MAPLE NUT CAKE

1/3 cup shortening
1 cup light brown sugar
2 eggs
1 teaspoon vanilla extract
1/2 cup milk
1-1/2 cups flour
1/4 teaspoon salt
2 teaspoons Royal Baking Powder
1 cup chopped nuts—preferably pecans

Cream shortening, add sugar, egg yolks, flavoring and milk, and beat well; add flour, salt and baking powder which have been sifted together, and add chopped nuts; mix in beaten egg whites. Bake in greased loaf pan in moderate oven 35 to 45 minutes. Cover top with maple icing page 17. While still soft sprinkle with chopped nuts.

SOFT MOLASSES CAKE

1/2 cup shortening
2/3 cup brown sugar
1 egg
1/2 cup molasses
2 cups flour
3 teaspoons Royal Baking Powder
1/2 teaspoon salt

1/2 teaspoon allspice
1/2 teaspoon cinnamon
2/3 cup milk

Cream shortening. Add sugar slowly; beating continually; add beaten egg and molasses; add half of flour, baking powder, salt and spices which have been sifted together; mix and add milk and remainder of dry ingredients. Mix well. Bake in greased shallow pan in moderate oven about 40 minutes. Serve hot.

FAIRMOUNT CAKE

2 cups flour
2 teaspoons Royal Baking Powder
1/2 cup shortening
1-1/4 cups sugar
1/2 cup milk
1 teaspoon vanilla extract
3 eggs
1/2 cup fresh grated cocoanut

Sift flour and baking powder three times; beat shortening and sugar to a cream; add milk and vanilla, then flour, a little at a time; beat until smooth; add eggs one at a time, stirring and beating batter well after each egg is added. Bake in greased loaf pan in moderate oven 1 hour. Cover with boiled icing, page 16 and sprinkle with cocoanut.

MARBLE CAKE

WHITE PART

3 tablespoons shortening
1/2 cup sugar
1/2 teaspoon lemon extract
1/2 cup milk
1 cup flour
2 teaspoons Royal Baking Powder
1/4 teaspoon salt
white of 1 egg

Cream shortening; add sugar slowly; add flavoring and milk. Beat well and add flour sifted with baking powder and salt. Mix in beaten egg white.

DARK PART

3 tablespoons shortening
1/2 cup sugar
yolk of 1 egg
1/2 cup milk
1 cup flour
2 teaspoons Royal Baking Powder

1/4 teaspoon salt
1/2 teaspoon cloves
1/2 teaspoon allspice
1 teaspoon cinnamon
2 tablespoons cocoa

Cream shortening; add sugar slowly; add egg yolk and mix well. Mix in milk; add flour, baking powder, salt, spices and cocoa which have been sifted together. Put this batter by spoonfuls and same amount of white batter alternately into greased loaf pan but do not mix. Bake in moderate oven about 45 minutes. Cover with white icing, page 16.

MARBLE CAKE II

Make plain cake page 10; save one-third of batter and add to it 1-1/2 squares melted unsweetened chocolate. Drop by spoonfuls into white batter after putting in pan. Bake in moderate oven about 45 minutes.

FEATHER COCOANUT CAKE

1-1/2 cups flour
7/8 cup sugar
2 teaspoons Royal Baking Powder
2 tablespoons melted shortening
1 egg
1/2 cup milk
1 teaspoon lemon extract
1/2 cup fresh grated cocoanut

Sift flour, sugar and baking powder. Add shortening and beaten egg to milk and add to dry ingredients. Mix well, add flavoring and cocoanut and bake in greased loaf pan in moderate oven 35 to 45 minutes. Sprinkle with powdered sugar, or ice with white icing, page 16 with grated cocoanut sprinkled on top.

CHOCOLATE LAYER CAKE

1/3 cup shortening
1 cup sugar
1 egg
1 cup milk
1-3/4 cups flour
4 teaspoons Royal Baking Powder
1/4 teaspoon salt
1 teaspoon vanilla extract

Cream shortening; add sugar gradually, beating well; add beaten egg, one-half the milk and mix well; add one-half the flour which has been sifted with salt and baking powder; add remainder of milk, then remainder of flour and flavoring; beat after each addition. Bake in greased layer cake tins in moderate oven 15 to 20 minutes.

CHOCOLATE FILLING AND ICING

3 cups confectioner's sugar
boiling water
1 teaspoon vanilla extract
2 ounces unsweetened chocolate
1/2 teaspoon grated orange peel

To sugar add boiling water slowly to make a smooth paste; add vanilla, melted chocolate and orange peel. Spread between layers and on top of cake.

ORANGE LAYER CAKE

1/3 cup shortening
1 cup sugar
2 eggs
2/3 cup milk
1-3/4 cups flour
3 teaspoons Royal Baking Powder
1 teaspoon vanilla extract

Cream shortening; add sugar and egg yolks; mix well and add half the milk; add half the flour which has been sifted with baking powder; mix in flavoring, milk and remainder of flour. Bake in two greased layer cake tins in moderate oven about 20 minutes.

ORANGE FILLING AND ICING

whites of 2 eggs
1-1/2 cups confectioner's sugar
rind and soft pulp of 1 orange

Whip eggs to stiff froth; add sugar, a little at a time, until stiff enough to spread. Whip in pulp and rind of orange. Orange coloring may be added if desired.

WHITE LAYER CAKE

1/2 cup shortening
1 cup granulated sugar
1/2 cup cold water
2 cups flour
2 teaspoons Royal Baking Powder
whites of 3 eggs
1 teaspoon vanilla or almond extract

Cream shortening and sugar together until very light; add water slowly, almost drop by drop, and beat constantly; stir in flour and baking powder which have been sifted together twice; add flavoring; mix in egg whites which have been beaten until stiff. Bake in two greased layer cake tins in moderate oven 20 to 25 minutes. Put together with fresh strawberry or maple filling, page 17.

DEVIL'S FOOD CAKE

1/2 cup shortening
1 cup sugar
2-1/2 ounces chocolate
1/2 cup mashed potatoes
1 egg
3/8 cup milk
1-1/4 cups flour
2 teaspoons Royal Baking Powder
1/2 cup chopped nuts
1/2 teaspoon vanilla extract

Cream shortening; add sugar, melted chocolate and mashed potatoes; mix well; add egg yolk, milk and flour and baking powder which have been sifted together; beat well; add nuts, vanilla and beaten egg white; mix thoroughly. Bake in greased shallow tin in moderate oven 25 to 35 minutes.

MARSHMALLOW ICING

3/4 cup granulated sugar
1/3 cup water
6 or 8 marshmallows
white of 1 egg
few drops vanilla extract

Boil sugar and water without stirring until syrup spins a thread; melt marshmallows in syrup; pour slowly over beaten white of egg; add flavoring and spread *very thickly* over cake. Melt 2 ounces unsweetened chocolate with one-half teaspoon butter and spread thin coating over icing when cool.

CREAM LAYER CAKE

1/2 cup shortening
1 cup sugar
2 eggs
1 teaspoon vanilla extract
1/2 cup milk
2 cups flour
3 teaspoons Royal Baking Powder
1/4 teaspoon salt

Cream shortening and sugar together until light; add beaten egg yolks, flavoring and milk slowly; sift flour and salt; add half, then half beaten egg whites; add remainder of flour sifted with baking powder; stir after each addition; fold in remaining egg whites. Bake in greased layer cake tins in moderate oven 15 to 20 minutes. Put together with cream filling and cover top and sides with white icing.

CREAM FILLING

1 cup milk
2 tablespoons corn starch
1/4 teaspoon salt
2 tablespoons sugar
1 egg
1 teaspoon vanilla extract

Scald milk. Mix corn starch, salt and sugar with a little cold milk; add to beaten egg; then add to hot milk. Cook about three minutes or until thick and smooth; add flavoring, and spread between layers.

COCOANUT LAYER CAKE

1/4 cup shortening
1 cup sugar
1 teaspoon vanilla extract
1 egg
1 cup milk
2 cups flour
1/8 teaspoon salt
3 teaspoons Royal Baking Powder

Cream shortening, add sugar slowly, add flavoring and beaten egg; add milk; mix well; then add flour, salt and baking powder which have been sifted together. Bake in three greased layer cake tins in moderate oven 12 to 15 minutes.

COCOANUT FILLING AND ICING

1-1/2 cups granulated sugar
1/2 cup water
2 egg whites
1/2 teaspoon vanilla extract, few drops lemon juice
1 cup fresh grated cocoanut

Cook sugar and water slowly without stirring until syrup spins a thread; pour slowly over beaten egg whites; beat until thick; add flavoring. Spread between layers and on top of cake. While icing is soft sprinkle thickly with cocoanut.

MAPLE LAYER CAKE

1/2 cup shortening
1 cup sugar
2 eggs
1 teaspoon vanilla extract
1/2 cup milk
2 cups flour
3 teaspoons Royal Baking Powder
1/4 teaspoon salt

Cream shortening, and sugar; add egg yolks and flavoring; mix well; add milk slowly, stirring until smooth; sift flour, baking powder and salt together; add half to mixture, then half of beaten egg whites, then remainder of flour (stirring after each addition); mix in balance of whites. Bake in greased layer cake tins in moderate oven 12 to 15 minutes. For middle layer of chocolate, take 1-3 of batter of above recipe and add 1 oz. melted chocolate. Put together with maple icing, page 17.

FRUIT LAYER CAKE

1/3 cup shortening
1 cup sugar
1 egg
1 teaspoon vanilla extract
1 cup milk
2 cups flour
4 teaspoons Royal Baking Powder
1/8 teaspoon salt

Cream shortening well; add sugar; add yolk of egg and vanilla; mix well; add milk, then flour, baking powder and salt which have been sifted together; mix in beaten egg white. Bake in three greased layer tins in hot oven about 15 minutes. Put cake together with fruit filling and cover with white icing, page 16.

FRUIT FILLING

1/2 cup fruit jelly
1 cup water
1/2 cup chopped raisins
1/4 lb. chopped figs
1/4 cup sugar
2 tablespoons corn starch
1/2 cup chopped blanched almonds or walnuts
juice of 1/2 lemon

Cook jelly with water, fruit and sugar; add corn starch which has been mixed with a little cold water. Cook until thick, remove from fire; add nuts and lemon juice. Cool and spread between layers of cake.

LADY BALTIMORE CAKE

1/2 cup shortening
1 cup sugar
whites of 3 eggs
1/2 cup milk
1 teaspoon vanilla extract or 1/2 teaspoon almond extract
1-3/4 cups flour
2 teaspoons Royal Baking Powder

Cream shortening; add sugar and unbeaten white of one egg; add milk very slowly, beating between each addition; add flavoring; add flour which has been sifted with baking powder; lastly fold in beaten whites of 2 eggs. Bake in square greased layer tins in hot oven about 15 minutes. Use following filling and cover top and sides of cake with white icing, page 16.

FILLING

1-1/2 cups sugar
1/2 cup water
whites of 2 eggs
1/2 cup chopped seeded raisins
1/2 cup chopped figs
1 cup chopped blanched almonds or pecan nuts
1/2 teaspoon vanilla extract

Boil sugar and water without stirring until syrup spins a thread. Pour syrup slowly over beaten eggs. Mix in fruit, nuts and flavoring. Spread between layers of cake.

SPONGE CAKE

6 eggs
1 cup granulated sugar
rind of half a lemon
2 tablespoons lemon juice
1 cup flour
1 teaspoon Royal Baking Powder
1/2 teaspoon salt

Beat egg yolks with wire whip until thick; add gradually sifted sugar, then grated lemon rind, lemon juice and one-half beaten whites; mix well; carefully fold in flour which has been sifted with baking powder and salt; add remainder of whites, mix lightly and bake in ungreased sponge cake tin in moderate oven 35 to 45 minutes. When cake shrinks from pan remove from oven and turn upside down on cake cooler.

ROYAL SPONGE CAKE

1 cup sugar
1/2 cup water
3 eggs
1 cup flour
1/2 teaspoon salt
2 teaspoons Royal Baking Powder
1 teaspoon vanilla or lemon extract
1/8 cup cold water

Boil sugar and water without stirring until syrup spins a thread and add slowly to beaten egg whites, beating until mixture is cold; sift together three times, flour, salt and baking powder; beat egg yolks until thick; add a little at a time, flour mixture and egg yolks, alternately to white of egg mixture; add cold water and flavoring; mix lightly. Bake in ungreased tin in moderate, oven about one hour.

MILK SPONGE CAKE

2 eggs
1 cup sugar
6 tablespoons hot milk
1 teaspoon vanilla or lemon extract
1 cup flour
1-1/2 teaspoons Royal Baking Powder
1/8 teaspoon salt

Beat egg yolks until thick; add half the sugar, beating continually; add hot milk, remainder of sugar and beaten egg whites; add flavoring; add flour, salt and baking powder which have been sifted together. Bake in ungreased tube pan in moderate oven about 25 minutes.

COFFEE SPICE CAKE WITH MOCHA FILLING

1/2 cup shortening
1 cup sugar
2 eggs
1/2 cup strong coffee
2 cups flour
3 teaspoons Royal Baking Powder
1/8 teaspoon salt
2 teaspoons mixed spices

Cream shortening and sugar until light; add beaten egg yolks; add coffee slowly; add half the flour sifted with baking powder, salt and spices; mix well and add beaten egg whites; add remainder of flour and mix lightly. Bake in greased layer cake tins in moderate oven 45 to 50 minutes. Spread layers and cover top with

MOCHA ICING AND FILLING

1 tablespoon butter
1 cup confectioner's sugar
1 tablespoon cocoa
2 tablespoons strong coffee
1/4 teaspoon salt

Cream butter and sugar; add cocoa, coffee and salt and stir until smooth. If too dry, add more coffee.

ICINGS AND FILLINGS

BOILED ICING

1 cup granulated sugar
1/2 cup water
white of 1 egg
1/2 teaspoon flavoring extract
1 teaspoon Royal Baking Powder

Boil sugar and water without stirring until syrup spins a thread; pour very slowly over stiffly beaten egg white and beat until smooth; add flavoring and baking powder; allow to stand few minutes before spreading.

FROSTING

1 unbeaten egg white
1-1/2 cups confectioner's sugar
1 teaspoon vanilla extract

Put egg white into shallow dish; add sugar gradually, beating with wire whip until of right consistency to spread; add vanilla and spread on cake.

ORNAMENTAL FROSTING

1-1/2 cups granulated sugar
1/2 cup water
2 egg whites
1 teaspoon flavoring extract
1 teaspoon Royal Baking Powder

Boil sugar and water without stirring until syrup spins a thread; add very slowly to beaten egg whites; add flavoring and baking powder and beat until smooth and stiff enough to spread. Put over boiling water, stirring continually until icing grates slightly on bottom of bowl. Spread on cake saving a small portion of icing to ornament the edge of cake. This can be forced through a pastry tube, or, through a cornucopia, made from ordinary white letter paper.

WHITE OR COLORED ICING

1-1/2 cups confectioner's sugar
2 tablespoons hot milk
1/2 teaspoon butter

1/2 teaspoon vanilla extract

Add butter to hot milk; add sugar slowly to make right consistency to spread; add vanilla. Spread on cake.

For pink icing add one tablespoon strawberry or other fruit juice. For yellow icing add one teaspoon egg yolk and flavor with orange rind and one teaspoon lemon juice.

SEVEN MINUTE ICING

1 unbeaten egg white
7/8 cup granulated sugar
3 tablespoons cold water

Place all ingredients in top of double boiler. Place over boiling water and beat with beater for seven minutes. Add 1/2 teaspoon flavoring and spread on cake.

For "Chocolate Icing" add to above 1-1/2 ounces melted unsweetened chocolate.

For "Coffee Icing" add 3 tablespoons cold boiled coffee in place of water.

CHOCOLATE FILLING AND ICING

whites of 2 eggs
2 cups confectioner's sugar
1-1/2 tablespoons milk
1 teaspoon vanilla extract
4 ounces chocolate
1 teaspoon butter

Beat whites until stiff; add sugar slowly, beating well; add milk, vanilla and chocolate which has been melted with butter; mix until smooth. Spread on cake.

OLD-FASHIONED CHOCOLATE FILLING

3 ounces melted chocolate
3 tablespoons cream
1 egg
3/4 cup powdered sugar
1 tablespoon corn starch
1/8 teaspoon salt
1 teaspoon vanilla extract

Add melted chocolate and cream to beaten egg; mix in powdered sugar gradually; add corn starch which has been mixed with a little cold water; cook in top of double boiler, stirring constantly until smooth and thick; add salt and vanilla. Spread between layers of cake.

SOFT ICING

2/3 cup light syrup

1/3 cup granulated sugar
2 tablespoons cold water
whites of 2 eggs
1 teaspoon corn starch
1/2 teaspoon Royal Baking Powder
1 teaspoon vanilla extract

Boil syrup, sugar and water without stirring until syrup spins a thread; pour slowly into stiffly beaten egg whites and beat well. Add corn starch, baking powder and flavoring, and mix until smooth.

MARSHMALLOW FILLING AND ICING

1-3/4 cups sugar
1/8 teaspoon salt
1/2 cup water
1/2 cup marshmallows
whites of 3 eggs

Mix sugar, salt and water, add marshmallows and boil until syrup spins a thread, then add slowly to beaten egg whites; beat until firm enough to spread.

FRUIT FILLING

2 cups granulated sugar
2/3 cup boiling water
whites of 2 eggs
1/4 cup chopped nuts
1 cup mixed figs, raisins, citron, cherries and pine apple, cut fine

Boil sugar and water without stirring until syrup spins a thread; beat whites until dry; add syrup gradually, beating constantly; when cool add nuts and fruit. Spread between layers of cake.

FRESH STRAWBERRY ICING

Crush ten strawberries with a little sugar and few drops lemon juice and let stand until juicy; mix in gradually three cups of confectioner's sugar. Spread between layers and on top of cake.

MAPLE ICING. I

1/2 teaspoon butter
2 tablespoons hot milk
1-1/2 cups confectioner's sugar
1/2 teaspoon maple flavoring

Add butter to hot milk; add sugar slowly to make paste of the right consistency to spread; add flavoring and spread on cake.

MAPLE ICING. II

1 cup maple syrup
whites of 2 eggs

Boil syrup without stirring until it spins a thread; add slowly to stiffly beaten egg whites; beat with wire whip, preferably on platter, until stiff enough to spread.

ORANGE ICING

rind of 1 orange
2 teaspoons lemon juice
1 cup confectioner's or powdered sugar
white of 1 egg

Grate orange rind and allow gratings to soak for some time in lemon juice; stir juice, sugar and egg together and beat thoroughly. Spread on warm cake.

JELLY MERINGUE

white of 1 egg
1/2 cup currant or other jelly

Put egg white and jelly together into bowl and beat with egg beater or wire whip until stiff. Spread between layers or on top of cake.

SEA FOAM ICING

1 cup brown sugar
1/3 cup water
white of 1 egg
1 teaspoon Royal Baking Powder

Boil sugar and water without stirring until syrup spins a thread. Add hot syrup slowly to beaten egg white, beating continually, preferably on platter with wire whip. Add baking powder. When icing foams, put between layers and on top of cake.

COCOA ICING

1 cup confectioner's sugar
4 tablespoons cocoa
1 egg white
1 teaspoon vanilla extract
1 tablespoon cream
1 teaspoon melted butter

Add sugar and cocoa slowly to beaten egg white. Then add vanilla, melted butter and cream to make soft enough to spread on cake.

BROWN SUGAR ICING AND FILLING

3 cups brown sugar
1 cup milk
1 tablespoon butter
1 teaspoon vanilla extract

Cook sugar, milk and butter together until it forms a soft ball when tested in cold water; add vanilla. Beat until thick and spread on cake. Chopped nuts can be added if desired.

BUTTER SCOTCH ICING AND FILLING (WITHOUT SUGAR)

2 cups light syrup
1/2 cup butter
1/2 cup milk

Boil syrup, butter and milk together until it forms a soft ball when tested in cold water. Cool slightly without stirring and pour while warm on cake.

Chopped nuts may be added while icing is still soft.

COOKIES AND SMALL CAKES

COCOA DROP CAKES

4 tablespoons shortening
1 cup sugar
1 egg
1/2 cup milk
1-3/4 cups flour
3 teaspoons Royal Baking Powder
1/2 cup cocoa
1/4 teaspoon salt
1 teaspoon vanilla extract

Cream shortening; add sugar and beaten egg; beat well and add milk slowly; sift flour, baking powder, salt and cocoa into mixture; stir until smooth; add vanilla. Put one tablespoon of batter into each greased muffin tin and bake in moderate oven about 20 minutes. Cover with boiled icing, page 16.

Or bake in shallow pan; cool, and before removing cut across diagonally to make diamond-shaped pieces; cover with icing.

RAISIN DROP CAKES

4 tablespoons shortening
1 cup sugar
1 egg
2/3 cup milk
1-3/4 cups flour
3 teaspoons Royal Baking Powder
1/8 teaspoon salt
1 cup raisins
1 teaspoon vanilla extract

Cream shortening; add sugar; add beaten egg and milk very slowly; add flour, baking powder and salt which have been sifted together; add raisins which have been washed, drained and floured slightly; add flavoring, mix well. Put a small amount of mixture into each greased individual cake tin and bake in hot oven 15 to 20 minutes. Sprinkle with powdered sugar, or cover with icing.

ORANGE CAKES

4 tablespoons shortening
1 cup sugar
2/3 cup milk
1 egg
2 cups flour
3 teaspoons Royal Baking Powder
1/8 teaspoon salt
1 teaspoon orange extract
grated rind of 1 orange

Cream shortening; add sugar slowly beating well; add milk a little at a time; add beaten egg; sift flour, baking powder and salt together and add to mixture; add flavoring and grated orange rind; mix well. Bake in greased shallow tin, or individual cake tins, in hot oven 15 to 20 minutes. When cool cover with orange icing, page 17.

SPICE CAKES

1/2 cup shortening
1 cup brown sugar
1 egg
1-3/4 cups flour
3 teaspoons Royal Baking Powder
1/2 teaspoon cinnamon
1/4 teaspoon nutmeg
1/4 teaspoon cloves
1/2 cup milk
1 cup chopped raisins

Cream shortening, add sugar and beaten egg; add flour, baking powder and spices which have been sifted together; add milk and mix well; mix in raisins which have been slightly floured. Bake in small greased tins in moderate oven about 25 minutes.

HONEY DROP CAKES

1/3 cup shortening
1/4 cup sugar
1/2 cup honey
1 egg
1/2 tablespoon lemon juice
1-1/2 cups flour
1-1/2 teaspoons Royal Baking Powder

Cream shortening and add sugar slowly; add honey, beaten egg yolk and lemon juice; mix well and add flour and baking powder which have been sifted together; fold in beaten egg white. Put into greased individual tins or drop far apart on greased baking sheet and bake in hot oven 10 to 15 minutes.

MOLASSES CAKES

1 cup molasses
1/2 cup sugar
1/2 cup melted shortening
1/2 cup boiling water
3 cups flour
3 teaspoons Royal Baking Powder
1 teaspoon salt
1/2 teaspoon soda
2 teaspoons cinnamon
1 teaspoon nutmeg
1 teaspoon cloves
1 cup stale bread crumbs

Mix molasses, sugar, shortening and boiling water together; add flour, baking powder, salt, soda and spices which have been sifted together; add bread crumbs; mix well. Drop by spoonfuls on greased baking sheet and bake in moderate oven 10 to 12 minutes.

SMALL FANCY CAKES. I

1/2 cup shortening
1 cup granulated or powdered sugar
yolks of 3 eggs
1/2 cup milk
2 cups flour
2 teaspoons Royal Baking Powder

Cream shortening, add sugar slowly and beat well; add beaten egg yolks; add milk a little at a time and flour which has been sifted with baking powder; divide batter in half and add to one-half, one teaspoon lemon juice and grated rind of half a lemon; to remainder of batter add two ounces unsweetened melted chocolate, one teaspoon vanilla. Bake in shallow greased pan or in small individual tins in hot oven about 15 minutes. If large pan is used, when cool, cut cakes into fancy shapes. Cakes should be less than an inch thick when baked. Spread with colored icing, page 16, or marshmallow icing, page 17.

SMALL FANCY CAKES. II

1/2 cup shortening
1 cup granulated sugar
2/3 cup water
1 teaspoon vanilla extract
2 cups flour
1/4 teaspoon salt
3 teaspoons Royal Baking Powder
whites of 3 eggs

Cream shortening and sugar together until very light; add water very slowly and beat constantly; add flavoring; stir in the flour, salt and baking powder which have been sifted together twice; mix in beaten egg whites. Put about a teaspoonful of batter into small individual cake tins and bake in hot oven 10 to 15 minutes, or bake in shallow pan and cut as in above recipe or diagonally across making small diamond shaped pieces. Spread with any icing desired.

COOKIES

    3/4 cup shortening
    2 cups sugar
    1/4 cup milk
    2 eggs
    1/4 teaspoon grated nutmeg
    1 teaspoon vanilla or grated
    rind of 1 lemon
    4 cups flour
    3 teaspoons Royal Baking Powder

Cream shortening and sugar together; add milk to beaten eggs and beat again; add slowly to creamed shortening and sugar; add flavoring; add 2 cups flour sifted with baking powder and nutmeg; add enough more flour to roll easily. Roll out very thin on floured board; cut with cookie cutter; sprinkle with sugar; put a raisin or a piece of walnut in the center of each. Bake about 12 minutes in hot oven.

COCOA COOKIES

    4 tablespoons shortening
    1 cup sugar
    1/4 cup milk
    1 egg
    2 cups flour
    3 teaspoons Royal Baking Powder
    1/4 teaspoon salt
    1/2 cup cocoa

Cream shortening and sugar together; add milk and beaten egg; mix well. Sift flour, baking powder, cocoa and salt together and add. Roll out 1/4-inch thick on floured board; cut with cookie cutter. Bake in hot oven about 12 minutes.

COCOANUT COOKIES

    1/4 cup shortening
    1/2 cup sugar
    1 egg
    1/2 teaspoon lemon juice or extract
    1/2 cup milk
    1-1/2 cups flour
    3 teaspoons Royal Baking Powder
    1/8 teaspoon salt

2 cups fresh grated cocoanut

Cream shortening; add sugar, beaten egg and lemon; mix in milk slowly; add flour, baking powder and salt which have been sifted together; add cocoanut. The batter should be quite stiff. Drop by small spoonfuls on greased pan. Do not smooth over, but allow space for spreading. Bake in moderate oven 15 to 20 minutes.

FILLED COOKIES

1/3 cup shortening
1 cup sugar
1 egg
1/2 cup milk
1 teaspoon vanilla extract
3-1/2 cups flour
1/2 teaspoon salt
4 teaspoons Royal Baking Powder

Cream shortening; add sugar, beaten egg, milk and vanilla; add flour, salt and baking powder, which have been sifted together. Roll out thin on slightly floured board and cut with cookie cutter. Place one teaspoon of filling on each cookie, cover with another cookie, press edges together. Bake in moderate oven 12 to 15 minutes.

FILLING

2 teaspoons flour
1/2 cup sugar
1/2 cup water
1/2 cup chopped raisins
1/2 cup chopped figs

Mix flour and sugar together; add water and fruit. Cook until thick, being very careful not to burn.

MARSHMALLOW COOKIES

Follow recipe for cookies. Roll slightly thicker. After removing from oven, cover with marshmallow icing, page 17.

FUDGE SQUARES

3 tablespoons shortening
1 cup sugar
1 egg
2 ounces melted unsweetened chocolate
1/2 teaspoon vanilla extract
1/3 cup milk
1 cup flour

1 teaspoon Royal Baking Powder
1/8 teaspoon salt
1/2 cup nut meats chopped—not too fine

Melt shortening; add sugar and unbeaten egg; mix well; add chocolate, vanilla and milk; add flour which has been sifted with baking powder and salt; add nut meats, mix well. Spread thinly on greased shallow cake pan, and bake in slow oven 20 to 30 minutes. Cut into 2-inch squares before removing from pan.

OATMEAL MACAROONS

1 cup sugar.
1 tablespoon melted shortening
2 eggs
3/4 teaspoon salt
2-1/2 cups rolled oats
2 teaspoons Royal Baking Powder
1 teaspoon vanilla extract

Cream sugar with shortening; add egg yolks, salt and rolled oats; add baking powder, beaten egg whites and vanilla; mix thoroughly. Drop on greased tins about half teaspoon to each macaroon allowing space for spreading. Bake about 10 minutes in moderate oven.

HERMITS

6 tablespoons shortening
1 cup brown sugar
1 egg
1/2 cup milk
1-1/2 cups flour
2 teaspoons Royal Baking Powder
1/4 teaspoon salt
1 teaspoon cloves
1 teaspoon allspice
1 teaspoon cinnamon
1 cup chopped seeded raisins
2 tablespoons chopped citron

Cream shortening; add sugar and beaten egg; mix well; add milk very slowly; sift flour, baking powder, salt and spices together and add slowly; add fruit dredged with flour. Drop from spoon on greased tins and bake in moderate oven 15 minutes.

NUT BARS

1/2 cup shortening
1-1/2 cups sugar
2 eggs
4 tablespoons milk

4 cups flour
3 teaspoons Royal Baking Powder
1/8 teaspoon salt
1/2 cup chopped blanched almonds

Cream shortening and sugar together; add beaten yolk of one egg; add beaten whites of two eggs and three tablespoons milk; mix well. Sift together flour, baking powder and salt and add, mixing well. Roll half of dough at a time 1/4-inch thick on floured board; cut into bars 1 by 3 inches. Brush with yolk of remaining egg mixed with one tablespoon milk and sprinkle with chopped nuts. Bake in moderate oven about 15 minutes.

FRUIT SHORTCAKES

Although strawberries are generally used, other fruits such as raspberries, blackberries, loganberries, bananas, peaches and oranges, and even stewed or canned fruit, can be substituted and make delicious short cakes.

OLD-FASHIONED SHORTCAKE

2 cups flour
1/2 teaspoon salt
2 tablespoons sugar
4 teaspoons Royal Baking Powder
3 tablespoons shortening
3/4 cup milk
1 quart berries

Sift dry ingredients; mix in shortening; add milk to make soft dough; smooth out lightly. Bake in greased deep layer cake tin in hot oven 20 to 25 minutes. Split, butter and spread sweetened crushed berries or other fruit between layers.

STRAWBERRY SHORTCAKE

2 cups flour
1/2 teaspoon salt
2 tablespoons sugar
4 teaspoons Royal Baking Powder
3 tablespoons shortening
1 egg
1/2 cup milk

Sift dry ingredients, mix in shortening; add beaten egg to milk and add to dry ingredients to make soft dough. Smooth one half of dough out lightly. Put into greased deep layer tin; spread with butter; cover with other half of dough which has also been smoothed out to fit pan. Bake in hot oven 20 to 25 minutes. Split while hot and spread crushed and sweetened berries and whipped cream between layers; cover top with whipped cream and whole berries. Dust with powdered sugar and serve.

ROYAL STRAWBERRY CAKE

1 cup sugar
4 tablespoons shortening

1 egg
2 cups flour
3 teaspoons Royal Baking Powder
1/8 teaspoon salt
1 cup milk
1 teaspoon vanilla extract
1/2 pint heavy cream
1 quart strawberries

Cream sugar and shortening together; add beaten egg; add part of flour, baking powder and salt which have been sifted together, then part of milk; mix well and add remainder of flour; mix in remainder of milk and flavoring. Bake in shallow greased pan in moderate oven 20 to 30 minutes. When cold split in half and spread whipped cream and crushed sweetened strawberries between layers. Cover top with whipped cream and whole strawberries.

DOUGHNUTS

These old-fashioned "fried cakes," as sometimes called, need the addition of Royal Baking Powder to make them light, tender and digestible. The fat should be in a deep kettle, and hot enough to brown a piece of bread in 60 seconds or the doughnuts will absorb grease.

DOUGHNUTS

3 tablespoons shortening
2/3 cup sugar
1 egg
2/3 cup milk
1 teaspoon nutmeg
3/4 teaspoon salt
3 cups flour
4 teaspoons Royal Baking Powder

Cream shortening; add sugar and beaten egg; stir in milk; add nutmeg, salt, flour and baking powder which have been sifted together and enough additional flour to make dough stiff enough to roll. Roll out on floured board to about 1/4-inch thick; cut out. Fry in deep fat hot enough to brown a piece of bread in 60 seconds. Drain on unglazed paper and sprinkle with powdered sugar.

AFTERNOON TEA DOUGHNUTS

2 eggs
6 tablespoons sugar
3/4 teaspoon salt
1/4 teaspoon grated nutmeg
2 tablespoons melted shortening
6 tablespoons milk
2 cups flour
3 teaspoons Royal Baking Powder

Beat eggs until very light; add sugar, salt, nutmeg, shortening and milk; add flour and baking powder which have been sifted together; mix well. Drop by teaspoonfuls into deep hot fat and fry until brown. Drain well on unglazed paper and sprinkle with powdered sugar.

CRULLERS

4 tablespoons shortening
1 cup sugar
2 eggs
3 cups flour
1 teaspoon cinnamon
1/2 teaspoon salt
3 teaspoons Royal Baking Powder
5/8 cup milk

Cream shortening; add gradually sugar and beaten eggs; sift together flour, cinnamon, salt and baking powder; add one-half and mix well; add milk and remainder of dry ingredients to make soft dough. Roll out on floured board to about 1/2 inch thick and cut into strips about 4 inches long and 1/2 inch wide; roll in hands and twist each strip bringing ends together. Fry in deep fat. Drain and roll in powdered sugar.

PUDDINGS AND OTHER DESSERTS

BAKED CUSTARD

4 eggs
1/2 cup sugar
1/4 teaspoon salt
1 teaspoon vanilla extract
1 quart milk

Beat eggs, sugar, salt and vanilla together; scald milk and add very slowly, stirring constantly. Put into greased baking dish or small molds; place in pan of water in slow oven and bake 30 to 40 minutes. Test with knife which will come out clean when custard is baked.

For Caramel Custard add to eggs 4 tablespoons Caramel Sauce, page 26.

RICE PUDDING

1 cup rice
1-1/2 quarts milk
1 teaspoon salt
1 cup sugar
1 cup seeded raisins
grated orange rind

Wash rice with several waters; put into pudding dish; add milk, salt, orange rind and sugar and bake in slow oven about 1-1/2 hours or until thick, stirring several times during baking; add raisins, and bake 20 minutes longer.

COTTAGE PUDDING

1 cup flour
1/2 cup sugar
1/8 teaspoon salt
2 teaspoons Royal Baking Powder
1/2 cup milk
1 egg
2 tablespoons melted shortening

Sift together flour, sugar, salt and baking powder; add milk, beaten egg and shortening; beat well and bake in greased pan in hot oven about 20 minutes. Serve with lemon, chocolate or other sauce.

TAPIOCA PUDDING

1/2 cup pearl tapioca or 3 tablespoons minute tapioca
1 quart milk
1 teaspoon melted butter
6 tablespoons sugar
1/4 teaspoon salt
2 eggs
1 teaspoon vanilla or lemon extract

Soak tapioca in cold water one hour; drain; add milk and butter, and cook in double boiler until tapioca is transparent. Add sugar and salt to beaten eggs and combine by pouring hot mixture slowly on eggs. Return to double boiler and cook until thick. Add flavoring and serve hot or cold with cream.

POOR MAN'S PUDDING

1/2 cup chopped suet
1/2 cup seeded raisins
1/2 cup currants
1-1/2 cups grated bread
1 cup flour
2 teaspoons Royal Baking Powder
1/2 cup brown sugar
2 cups milk

Mix ingredients in order given; beat well. Put into greased mold; place in covered saucepan with boiling water half way up sides of mold. Steam 2 hours. Turn out carefully. Serve with hard or other sauce, page 25.

APPLE CAKE

1-1/2 cups flour
3 teaspoons Royal Baking Powder
1/2 teaspoon salt
2 tablespoons shortening
1/2 cup milk
4 or 5 apples
1/2 cup sugar
1 teaspoon cinnamon

Sift together flour, baking powder and salt; rub in shortening very lightly; add milk and mix. Place dough on floured board and pat out 1/2 inch thick. Put into shallow greased pan. Wash, pare, core and cut apples into sections; press them into dough; sprinkle with sugar and dust with cinnamon. Bake in moderate oven 30 minutes or until apples are tender and brown. Serve warm with milk or cream.

APPLE DUMPLINGS

1 cup flour

    2 teaspoons Royal Baking Powder
    1/2 teaspoon salt
    3 tablespoons shortening
    1/2 cup milk
    4 apples
    4 tablespoons sugar
    2 teaspoons butter
    1 teaspoon cinnamon

Sift together flour, baking powder and salt; rub shortening in lightly; add just enough milk to make a dough. Roll out 1/8 inch thick on floured board; divide into four parts; lay on each part an apple which has been washed, pared, cored and sliced; put one teaspoon sugar with 1/4 teaspoon butter on each; wet edges of dough with cold water and fold around apple, pressing tightly together. Place in pan, sprinkle with little cinnamon, remainder of sugar and put 1/4 teaspoon butter on each dumpling. Bake about 40 minutes in moderate oven. Serve with hard sauce, page 25.

Peach dumplings may be made in the same way.

APPLE ROLL

    4 medium sized apples
    1-1/2 cups sugar
    2 cups water

Peel, core and chop apples fine. Cook sugar and water in baking pan over slow fire. While cooking make rich biscuit dough (see strawberry shortcake, **page 21**). Roll out about 1/2-inch thick, spread with apples and roll into a long roll; cut into pieces about 1-1/2 or 2 inches long; place with cut side down in hot syrup; sprinkle with cinnamon and sugar and put small piece of butter on top of each. Bake in hot oven until apples are done and crust golden brown. Turn out on platter. Serve with plain or whipped cream. Peaches or other fruit may be used in place of apples.

MERINGUES

    whites of 3 eggs
    1-1/4 cups granulated sugar
    3 teaspoons Royal Baking Powder
    1/4 teaspoon vanilla extract

Beat whites of eggs until stiff and dry; add gradually two-thirds of sugar, and continue beating until mixture holds shape; fold in remaining sugar sifted with baking powder; add vanilla. Drop by spoonfuls on unglazed paper and bake in moderate oven 30 minutes. Increase heat and bake 30 minutes longer. Remove any soft part from center of meringues and return to oven to dry out, after turning off heat. Use two meringues for each serving and put together with ice cream or with sweetened whipped cream and crushed raspberries or strawberries.

BANANA CAKE WITH JELLY SAUCE

1 cup flour
2 teaspoons Royal Baking Powder
2 tablespoons sugar
1/4 teaspoon salt
3/4 cup milk
1 egg
4 bananas

Sift together the flour, baking powder, sugar and salt; add milk and beaten egg; mix well. Peel and scrape bananas; cut in halves, lengthwise, then across. Pour batter into greased shallow pan, place bananas on top and sprinkle with sugar. Bake in moderate oven 15 minutes. Serve with

JELLY SAUCE

1 cup water
2 tablespoons jelly
1 tablespoon sugar
1 teaspoon corn starch

Put water into saucepan; bring to a boil; add jelly and sugar; stir until dissolved; add corn starch wet with a little cold water; boil 3 minutes.

CHARLOTTE RUSSE

1 pint cream
1/4 cup powdered sugar
1 teaspoon vanilla extract

Mix ingredients. Have very cold and whip to stiff froth. Line dish with sponge cake or lady fingers, fill with whipped cream and serve cold.

BOSTON CREAM PIE

2 eggs
1 cup flour
1-1/2 teaspoons Royal Baking Powder
3/4 cup sugar
1/8 teaspoon salt
1/2 cup boiling milk
1/2 teaspoon vanilla extract

Add beaten egg yolks to stiffly beaten whites and gradually add flour, baking powder, sugar and salt which have been sifted together three or four times; add hot milk very slowly; add vanilla. Bake in deep layer cake tin in moderate oven about 35 minutes. When cool, split and put between layers the following cream filling. Sprinkle powdered sugar on top of cake.

CREAM FILLING

1/2 cup sugar

2 tablespoons corn starch
1/8 teaspoon salt
2 eggs
1 cup scalded milk
1 teaspoon butter
1/2 teaspoon vanilla extract

Mix sugar, corn starch, salt and beaten eggs; pour on gradually scalded milk; add butter; cook in double boiler until thick and smooth, stirring constantly; add flavoring; cool and spread between layers of cake.

BLUEBERRY CAKE

3 tablespoons shortening
1 cup sugar
1 egg
3/4 cup milk
1-3/4 cups flour
2 teaspoons Royal Baking Powder
1-1/2 cups floured blueberries

Cream shortening; add sugar, beaten egg and milk; sift flour and baking powder and add; stir in blueberries. Bake in very shallow greased pan in moderate oven 25 to 30 minutes. Serve hot with or without butter.

CHOCOLATE BLANC MANGE

4 tablespoons corn starch
3/4 cup sugar
1/4 teaspoon salt
1 quart milk
3 ounces unsweetened chocolate
1 teaspoon vanilla extract

Mix corn starch, sugar and salt together with a little of the cold milk. Put remainder of milk on to scald with chocolate, which has been cut into small pieces. As soon as chocolate is dissolved, stir in the corn starch mixture. Cook until thick and smooth, stirring constantly. Set over hot water and cook about 20 minutes longer. Add flavoring; pour into a mold which has been wet in cold water. Chill, and serve cold with sweetened whipped cream.

FLOATING ISLAND

1 quart milk
4 eggs
4 tablespoons sugar
1/4 teaspoon salt
1/2 cup currant jelly
2 teaspoons vanilla or almond extract

Scald milk; beat egg yolks; stir in sugar and salt; add hot milk gradually, mixing well. Cook slowly in saucepan until mixture begins to thicken, stirring continually. Cool, flavor and put into dish. Make meringue of whites whipped until dry, and into which jelly has been beaten, a teaspoon at a time, and heap on top; or drop meringue by spoonfuls on top of custard and put small pieces of jelly in center of each. Chill and serve.

HUCKLEBERRY OR BLUEBERRY FLOAT

1 cup berries
3 tablespoons sugar
1 cup flour
2 teaspoons Royal Baking Powder
1/4 teaspoon salt
1 teaspoon shortening
1/2 cup milk

Pick over and wash berries; put into small saucepan with half cup of water, and bring quickly to boil; add sugar and boil 5 minutes. Sift flour, baking powder and salt; mix in shortening very lightly; add milk slowly. Take a teaspoonful at a time in floured hands and roll into balls. Place on floured pie tin; brush with cold milk and bake about 12 minutes in hot oven. While warm break in half; butter each biscuit; put into dish and pour berries over. Serve hot with hard sauce.

CHRISTMAS PLUM PUDDING

2 cups ground suet
2 cups bread crumbs
2 cups flour
2 teaspoons Royal Baking Powder
2 cups sugar
2 cups seeded raisins
2 cups currants
1 cup finely cut citron
1 cup finely cut figs
1 tablespoon finely cut orange peel
1 tablespoon finely cut lemon peel
1 teaspoon ground cinnamon
1 teaspoon ground ginger
1/4 teaspoon ground cloves
1/4 teaspoon ground nutmeg
1/4 teaspoon ground mace
1 tablespoon salt
1 cup water
1 cup grape or other fruit juice

Mix thoroughly all dry ingredients and add fruit; stir in water and fruit juice and mix thoroughly. Add more water if necessary to make stiff dough. Fill greased molds 2/3 full, and steam five or six hours. This pudding should be prepared and cooked a week or more before used. Before serving steam one hour and serve with hard, lemon or foamy sauce.

CREAM PUFFS

    1 cup boiling water
    1/2 cup shortening
    1 cup flour
    1/8 teaspoon salt
    3 eggs
    2 teaspoons Royal Baking Powder

Heat water and shortening in saucepan until it boils up well; add all at once flour sifted with salt and stir vigorously. Remove from fire as soon as mixed, cool, and mix in unbeaten eggs, one at a time; add baking powder; mix and drop by spoonfuls 1-1/2 inches apart on greased tin; shape into circular form with wet spoon. Bake about 25 minutes in hot oven. Cut with sharp knife near base to admit filling.

CREAM FILLING

    1 cup sugar
    1/3 cup corn starch
    1/8 teaspoon salt
    1 egg
    2 cups scalded milk
    1 teaspoon vanilla extract

Mix dry ingredients; add slightly beaten egg and stir into this gradually the scalded milk. Cook about 15 minutes in double boiler, stirring constantly until thickened. Cool slightly and flavor.

Sweetened whipped cream may be used instead of this filling.

STEAMED FIG PUDDING

    1/4 cup shortening
    1 cup sugar
    1 egg
    1 cup milk
    2 cups flour
    4 teaspoons Royal Baking Powder
    1/8 teaspoon salt
    1/2 teaspoon vanilla or lemon extract
    1-1/2 cups chopped figs

Cream shortening; add sugar slowly and beaten egg; add milk; mix well; add flour, baking powder and salt, which have been sifted together; add flavoring and figs. Pour into greased pudding mold and steam for two hours. Serve with foamy sauce.

PRUNE PUFF

4 eggs
1/2 cup powdered sugar
1 cup cooked prunes

Whip egg whites to stiff froth; add sugar slowly, beating continually; add prunes which have been stoned and chopped; whip until very light. Bake in pudding dish in moderate oven about 10 minutes. Serve cold with soft custard made from yolks of eggs (see recipe for Floating Island, page 24).

Other soft fruits may be used in the same way served hot with sauce or whipped cream.

LEMON JELLY

1 cup sugar
1-1/2 cups water
1 tablespoon granulated gelatine
1/4 cup lemon juice

Boil sugar and water two or three minutes; add gelatine which has been soaked in two tablespoons cold water, stirring constantly; add lemon juice. Chill in mold which has been dipped in cold water and serve.

Fruit may be molded in the jelly by chilling part of mixture, adding fruit, then jelly; chilling and so on until mold is filled.

JELLY ROLL

1 cup sugar
1-1/2 cups flour
2 teaspoons Royal Baking Powder
1/8 teaspoon salt
2 eggs
4 tablespoons hot water
currant or other jelly

Sift dry ingredients; stir in beaten eggs; add hot water slowly; beat until smooth; pour into large well greased pan. Batter should be spread very thin and not more than 1/4 inch thick when baked. Bake in moderate oven 8 to 10 minutes. Turn out on sheet of brown paper; beat jelly with fork and spread on cake. With sharp knife trim off all crusty edges and roll up while still warm by lifting one side of paper. To keep roll perfectly round, wrap in slightly damp cloth until cool. Sprinkle with powdered sugar.

PUDDING SAUCES

HARD SAUCE

1/2 cup butter
1 cup powdered sugar
1/2 teaspoon flavoring extract

Cream butter until very light; add sugar very slowly, beating until light and creamy. Add flavoring and beat again.

FOAMY SAUCE

6 tablespoons butter
1 cup powdered sugar
3 eggs
1 teaspoon vanilla extract
2 tablespoons boiling water

Cream butter; add sugar slowly, beating continually; beat egg yolks until thick and add gradually; beat well; add stiffly beaten egg whites, flavoring and water. Before serving, heat over boiling water five minutes, stirring constantly.

CHOCOLATE SAUCE

1 ounce unsweetened chocolate
1 tablespoon butter
1/3 cup boiling water
1 cup sugar
1/2 teaspoon vanilla extract

Melt chocolate in top of double boiler. Add butter and when mixed pour water on slowly, stirring constantly, then add sugar. Bring to boiling point and boil about fifteen minutes, add vanilla, and serve hot.

MAPLE SAUCE

1 cup sugar
1 cup water
1 tablespoon lemon juice
1 tablespoon maple flavoring
1 teaspoon corn starch

Heat half the sugar in frying pan; stir continually; when brown add water and boil; add remainder of sugar, corn starch mixed with a little cold water, lemon juice and maple flavoring; boil 3 minutes. Serve hot.

LEMON OR ORANGE SAUCE

1 cup water
2 tablespoons lemon or orange juice
2 tablespoons sugar
1 teaspoons corn starch

Boil water, sugar and corn starch mixed with little cold water. Boil 5 minutes and add fruit juice and 1 tablespoon caramel if dark color is desired.

FRUIT SAUCE

1/3 cup butter
1 cup fresh strawberries, raspberries or canned fruit drained from syrup
1 cup powdered sugar
1 egg white

Cream butter; add sugar gradually; add egg beaten until stiff and beat well; add slowly fruit which has been carefully prepared and mashed. Beat until creamy.

CARAMEL SAUCE

2 cups granulated sugar
5 cups boiling water

Melt sugar in saucepan and heat, stirring constantly until golden brown; add boiling water. Cook three minutes.

PASTRY AND PIES

A pinch of salt and a little Royal Baking Powder make pastry light, flaky and more digestible.

Pastry should rise in baking to double its thickness, and be in light flaky layers. The novice must learn to handle it lightly and as little as possible in rolling and turning. It is important to have all materials and utensils cold.

Pastry is better if allowed to stand in the icebox several hours before using.

PLAIN PASTRY

2 cups flour
1/2 teaspoon salt
2 teaspoons Royal Baking Powder
1/2 cup shortening
cold water

Sift together flour, salt and baking powder; add shortening and rub in very lightly with tips of fingers. Add cold water very slowly, enough to hold dough together (do not work or knead dough and handle as little as possible). Divide in halves; roll out one part thin on floured board, and use for bottom crust. After pie is filled roll out other part for top. Cover pie; press edges together; trim off pastry and bake.

RICH PASTRY

2 cups pastry flour
1/2 teaspoon Royal Baking Powder
1/2 teaspoon salt
2/3 cup shortening
cold water

Sift flour, baking powder and salt; add one-half shortening and rub in lightly with fingers; add water slowly until of right consistency to roll out. Divide in halves; roll out one half thin; put on in small pieces half remaining shortening; fold upper and lower edges in to center; fold sides in to center; fold sides to center again; roll out thin and put loosely over pie plate, bringing paste well over edge of plate; trim off edges. Repeat with other half for top crust.

APPLE PIE

1-1/2 cups flour
1-1/2 teaspoons Royal Baking Powder
1/2 teaspoon salt
1/3 cup shortening
cold water
4 apples or 1 quart sliced apples
4 tablespoons sugar
1 tablespoon butter

Sift flour, baking powder and salt; add shortening and rub in very lightly; add just enough water to hold dough together. Roll half out on floured board, line bottom of pie plate; fill in apples, which have been washed, pared and cut into thin slices; sprinkle with sugar, and small pieces of butter; flavor with cinnamon or nutmeg; wet edges of crust with cold water; roll out remainder of pastry; cover pie, pressing edges tightly together, trim off extra pastry; prick top, and bake in moderate oven 30 minutes.

LEMON MERINGUE PIE

2 cups water
3 tablespoons corn starch
2 tablespoons flour
1 cup sugar
3 eggs
4 tablespoons lemon juice
1 teaspoon grated lemon rind
1 teaspoon salt

Line pie plate loosely with pastry and bake about 10 minutes or until very light brown. Put water on to boil; mix corn starch, flour and sugar with 1/2 cup cold water until smooth; add egg yolks; mix well and add slowly to boiling water. Cook 5 minutes, stirring constantly; add lemon juice, rind and salt. Pour into baked crust. Beat egg whites; add 3 tablespoons sugar and spread thickly over top of pie. Dust with sugar and brown in very slow oven.

STRAWBERRY PIE

1 cup flour
1/2 teaspoon salt
2 teaspoons Royal Baking Powder
4 tablespoons shortening
1/4 cup cold water
1 quart strawberries

Sift dry ingredients together; rub in shortening very lightly with finger tips; add water slowly to make a stiff dough. Roll out on floured board and use for bottom crust of pie, being careful to fold the paste well over the edge of pie plate. Bake in hot oven 12 to 15 minutes.

If glazed crust is desired, brush edges after baking with boiling hot syrup (2 tablespoons syrup and 1 tablespoon water) and return to oven for 1 or 2 minutes until syrup hardens. Fill the baked crust with fresh selected hulled strawberries and cover with syrup made as follows:

Add 1/2 cup sugar and 1/2 cup strawberries to 2 cups boiling water; bring to a boil and strain; add 1 tablespoon corn starch which has been mixed with little cold water. Cook over hot fire for a minute or two, stirring constantly; remove from fire and beat hard; return to slow fire, cook very gently until thick. Pour while hot over strawberries. Serve either hot or cold.

MINCE PIE

Mince Pie should always be made with two crusts. Line pie plate with paste, page 26, fill with mince meat, cover with paste and bake in hot oven 25 minutes.

MINCE MEAT

2 lbs. fresh lean beef, boiled and chopped fine when cold
1 lb. suet chopped very fine
5 lbs. chopped apples
1 lb. seeded raisins
2 lbs. currants
3/4 lb. sliced citron
1-1/2 teaspoons cinnamon
1 grated nutmeg
2 tablespoons ground mace
1 tablespoon ground cloves
1 tablespoon allspice
1 tablespoon fine salt
2-1/2 lbs. brown sugar
1 qt. sherry or 1 qt. boiled cider
1 pt. brandy

Mix all ingredients thoroughly. Pack in jars. Store in cold, dry place. Allow to stand 24 hours before using.

CUSTARD PIE

3 eggs
3/4 cup sugar
1 teaspoon salt
2 cups milk
1 teaspoon vanilla extract

Beat eggs; add sugar, salt and scalded milk slowly. Line pie plate with paste, page 26, pour in custard. Bake in moderate oven 25 to 30 minutes. The custard is baked when a knife put in center comes out dry.

Cocoanut Pie is made the same way, adding 1 cup fresh grated cocoanut, and using only 2 eggs. Bake as above.

PUMPKIN PIE

2 cups stewed and strained pumpkin
2 cups rich milk or cream
3/4 cup brown or granulated sugar
2 eggs
1/4 teaspoon ginger
1/2 teaspoon salt
1 teaspoon cinnamon

Mix pumpkin with milk, sugar, beaten eggs, ginger, salt, cinnamon, and beat 2 minutes. Pour into pie tin which has been lined with pastry. Place in hot oven for fifteen minutes, then reduce heat and bake 45 minutes in moderate oven.

RHUBARB PIE

2 cups rhubarb
1 cup sugar
1 tablespoon corn starch or flour
1/4 teaspoon salt

Cut off root, stem ends and peel; cut into small pieces; put into deep pie plate which has been lined with paste, **page 26**, sprinkle with corn starch, salt and sugar. Cover with paste and bake in hot oven about one-half hour.

BERRY PIES

3 cups blueberries, huckleberries, or blackberries
2/3 cup sugar
1/4 teaspoon salt
1 teaspoon flour
1 teaspoon butter

Line a pie plate with plain paste, **page 26**, fill heaping with berries; dredge with flour, salt and sugar; dot with small pieces of butter; cover with top crust or strips of pastry across top. Bake about 45 minutes in moderate oven.

Other fruit pies can be made in the same way.

CHERRY TARTS

1-1/2 cups flour
1/2 teaspoon salt
3 teaspoons Royal Baking Powder
6 tablespoons shortening
1/3 cup cold water
1 quart pitted cherries

Sift dry ingredients together; rub in shortening very lightly with fingertips; add water slowly, just enough to make stiff dough; roll out very thin on floured board and line patty pans, being very careful to have pastry come well over the edges of pans. Bake in hot oven about 12 or 15 minutes. Fill with cherries. Cover with hot syrup made as for strawberry pie, **page 27,** using 1/2 cup juice from the cherries instead of strawberries.

Other fruit can be used in place of cherries.

FROZEN DESSERTS

HOW TO FREEZE

Scald can, cover and dasher, adjust can in freezer; put in dasher; pour in the mixture to be frozen and fasten cover (the can should never be more than 3/4 full); adjust crank and turn once or twice. Fill space around can to within an inch of top with ice and salt (three parts crushed ice to one part salt), packing hard. Turn slowly at first, increasing speed when mixture begins to stiffen. Add more ice and salt as required. When mixture is very firm, wipe off cover, open can and remove dasher; scrape frozen mixture from dasher and sides of can, and pack down solidly; cover with paper and replace can cover. Put cork in opening in cover. Pour off salt water if there is danger of its getting into the can. Fill up over top of can with ice and salt (four parts ice to one part salt). Cover freezer with heavy blanket and keep in cool place until ready to serve.

PHILADELPHIA ICE CREAM

1 quart cream
1 cup sugar
1 tablespoon vanilla extract

Scald half pint of cream; add sugar and stir until dissolved. Cool and add remainder of cream and vanilla. Freeze as above.

STRAWBERRY ICE CREAM

Add to Philadelphia Ice Cream before freezing one quart of berries which have been washed, hulled, crushed and slightly sweetened.

CHOCOLATE ICE CREAM

Melt 2 ounces unsweetened chocolate with half pint cream and proceed as for Philadelphia Ice Cream.

FRENCH ICE CREAM

1 cup milk
yolks of 4 eggs
1 cup sugar
1/8 teaspoon salt
1 tablespoon vanilla extract

1 quart cream

Scald milk and add to beaten egg yolks; add sugar, salt, vanilla and cream which has been whipped. Freeze as above.

FROZEN PUDDING

3 cups milk
3 eggs
1 cup sugar
1 tablespoon corn starch
1 cup chopped mixed fruit

Scald milk in double boiler. Mix corn starch with a little cold milk; add beaten eggs, sugar and a few grains of salt; mix well and add slowly to scalded milk, stirring until it thickens. Cool and add fruit, which has been put through food chopper. The fruit is a matter of taste. It may be 2 tablespoons raisins, 1 tablespoon citron, 1 tablespoon cherries, 1 tablespoon blanched almonds and 1 tablespoon candied pineapple. Freeze, but not too stiff; put into mold and pack in ice and salt until ready to serve.

GRAPE SHERBET

1 pint grape juice
1 cup sugar
1 quart milk

Warm grape juice, and in it dissolve sugar; mix thoroughly with ice cold milk; freeze at once. This makes a lilac colored sherbet.

LEMON SHERBET

juice of 3 lemons
1-1/2 cups sugar
1 quart milk

Mix juice and sugar, stirring constantly while slowly adding very cold milk. If added too rapidly, mixture will curdle. However, this does not affect quality. Freeze and serve.

ORANGE WATER ICE

juice of 6 oranges
2 teaspoons orange extract
juice of 1 lemon
1 quart water
2 cups powdered sugar
1/2 cup cream

Mix all ingredients together; strain and freeze.

STRAWBERRY MOUSSE

1 box strawberries
1 cup sugar
1/4 box or 1 tablespoon granulated gelatine
2 tablespoons cold water
3 tablespoons boiling water
1 quart cream

Wash and hull berries, sprinkle with sugar and let stand one hour; mash and rub through fine sieve; add gelatine which has been soaked in cold water and dissolved in the boiling water. Set in pan of ice water and stir until it begins to thicken; fold in whipped cream. Put into mold, cover, pack in salt and ice, 1 part salt, 3 parts ice; allow to stand 4 hours. Raspberries or peaches or shredded pineapple may be used instead of strawberries.

SOUPS

Soup stock is the liquid in which bones, cooked or uncooked meat and vegetables have been boiled.

Gravies and browned pieces of meat are often added to the soup kettle for color and flavoring.

The stock should be strained, quickly cooled and all fat removed.

A great variety of soups may be made by adding to any soup stock, previously cooked macaroni, spaghetti, vermicelli noodles or vegetables.

Cream soups are made with a cream sauce foundation to which is added the strained pulp of vegetables or fish.

BROWN SOUP STOCK

6 lbs. shin of beef
3 to 6 quarts cold water
1 bay leaf
6 cloves
1 tablespoon mixed herbs
2 sprigs parsley
1/2 cup carrot
1/2 cup turnip
1/2 cup celery
1/2 cup onion

Wipe beef and cut lean meat into inch cubes; brown one-third in hot frying pan; put remaining two-thirds with bone and fat into soup kettle; add water and allow to stand 30 minutes. Place on back of range; add browned meat and heat gradually to boiling point. Cover and cook slowly six hours; add vegetables and seasoning one hour before it is finished. Strain and put away to cool. Remove all fat; reheat and serve.

BEAN SOUP

2 cups beans
2 tablespoons finely cut onion
2 tablespoons finely cut bacon
1 teaspoon salt
1/8 teaspoon pepper
2 tablespoons chopped parsley

1 teaspoon thyme
3 tablespoons flour

Soak beans in water over night. Drain and put into saucepan with six cups boiling water and boil slowly two hours or until soft; add onion and bacon which have been fried light brown; boil five minutes; add salt, pepper, parsley and thyme. Mash beans with back of spoon and add flour which has been mixed with a little cold water; boil five minutes and serve.

CREAM SOUPS

This is the foundation or sauce for many fish and vegetable cream soups.

1 quart milk
1 tablespoon butter
1 teaspoon salt
1 teaspoon white pepper
2 tablespoons flour
1 cup boiling water

Scald milk and add butter and seasoning; thicken with flour, which has been mixed with little cold water. Thin with boiling water and boil two minutes.

For pea soup boil and mash 1 pint green peas and add to sauce.

For cream of celery boil 1 pint cut celery until tender; rub through sieve, add to milk, and proceed as above.

For potato soup boil and mash 6 large potatoes, stir into milk, proceed as above, and strain. Just before serving stir in a tablespoon chopped parsley.

For corn soup add to sauce a can of corn or corn cut from 6 ears boiled fresh corn, 1 tablespoon sugar, and boil 15 minutes. Strain and serve.

For cream of fish soup add to milk about one pound of boiled fish, which has been put through sieve and proceed as above.

CREOLE SOUP

1/4 cup rice
1/2 cup cut onion
2 tablespoons bacon drippings
2 cups tomatoes
2 teaspoons salt
1 teaspoon sugar
1/8 teaspoon paprika
1 tablespoon cut parsley

Wash rice, add 3 cups boiling water and boil 30 minutes. Cook onions in pan with drippings until tender, but not brown; add tomatoes and boil 10 minutes; rub through strainer into boiled rice and water; add seasoning and sprinkle with parsley. Add a little chopped green pepper if desired.

CREAM OF TOMATO SOUP

1 quart tomatoes
1/4 teaspoon soda
4 tablespoons butter
4 tablespoons flour
1 quart milk
1 tablespoon salt
1/2 teaspoon pepper

Stew tomatoes slowly one-half hour. In the meantime, melt butter, stir in flour and cook over low flame, adding milk slowly; add seasoning. Strain tomatoes; add soda; stir into sauce and serve immediately.

ONION SOUP

2 cups finely chopped onion
2 tablespoons butter or bacon drippings
4 cups rice water or vegetable stock
1 teaspoon salt
1/8 teaspoon white pepper
1/8 teaspoon paprika
2 tablespoons chopped parsley

Cook onions and butter or drippings in covered saucepan, shaking pan often. When onions are tender add rice water or stock; boil 5 minutes; add seasoning and chopped parsley.

FISH

When a fish is fresh the flesh is firm and the gills are a bright pink.

To clean: Hold fish by the tail and with a sharp knife scrape off scales toward the head; wipe with damp cloth; slit underside; carefully remove entrails; wash with cold water, removing all clots of blood from backbone.

Always cook fish thoroughly.

BROILED FISH

Clean, wash, and split, removing backbone and fins along the edge. Very large fish should be cut into slices. Dry with cheesecloth; season with salt and pepper. Cook on well-greased broiler, from 10 to 20 minutes, turning once. Remove to hot platter; add melted butter and sprinkle with chopped parsley; garnish with slices of lemon and serve.

BAKED FISH

Prepare as for "Broiled fish." Brush pan with drippings; place fish, skin side down; dust with salt, pepper and flour; pour over 2 tablespoons melted butter and 1/2 cup milk. Bake in hot oven 20 to 25 minutes or until brown. Remove to hot platter, sprinkle with chopped parsley and serve.

FRIED FISH

Clean, removing head and tail, unless fish are small; wash with cold water and dry with cheesecloth; dust with salt, pepper and flour on both sides. Heat one tablespoon bacon drippings or other fat in heavy pan over hot fire. Put in fish; brown quickly on both sides; reduce heat and fry 5 to 10 minutes longer. Serve with chopped parsley and lemon or sauce tartare.

PLANKED FISH

Prepare as for "Broiled fish." Heat plank, brush with drippings and dust with salt and pepper. Place fish, skin side down, doubling thin part so that it will not burn. The oven must be hot before putting in plank; cook 20 minutes; reduce to moderate heat and leave in oven 10 to 20 minutes longer. Melt 1 tablespoon butter, add 1 teaspoon salt, 1/8 teaspoon pepper, and pour over fish. Garnish with potato roses, lemon and parsley and serve on the plank.

CODFISH BALLS

1 cup salt codfish
2 cups potatoes, cut into cubes or small pieces
1/8 teaspoon pepper
1/2 tablespoon butter
1 egg

Pick over, wash and shred fish into small pieces. Put potatoes into deep saucepan; cover with cold water; add fish and boil until potatoes are soft. Take off fire; drain well; beat up with wire whip or fork until light and all lumps are out of potatoes; add seasoning, butter and slightly beaten egg. Drop by spoonfuls into deep fat, hot enough to brown a piece of bread in 40 seconds and fry until golden brown. Drain on brown paper and serve immediately.

FISH CHOWDER

2 or 3 slices salt pork
6 medium-sized potatoes
1 small onion
3 lbs. fresh fish
2 quarts milk
2 teaspoons salt
1/8 teaspoon pepper

Cut pork in dice pieces; fry crisp, and turn into chowder kettle. Pare and cut potatoes into pieces. Peel and chop onion fine. Put potatoes into kettle with part of onion. Cut fish into convenient pieces; and lay over potatoes; sprinkle over with rest of onion; add seasoning and enough water to come to top of fish; cover closely and cook until potatoes are soft; add milk and let it scald up again. Pilot bread or crackers, split and soaked, may be added just before last boiling. If milk is not available a smaller quantity of water may be used.

BOILED LOBSTERS OR CRABS

The lobster should be purchased alive and plunged into boiling Water in which a good proportion of salt has been mixed. Continue to boil according to size about 20 minutes. Crabs should be boiled in the same manner, but only a little more than half the time is necessary.

To open a boiled lobster, wipe off shell, break off large claws; separate tail from body; take body from shell, leaving "lady" or stomach, on shell. Save green fat and coral; remove small claws; remove woolly gills and discard, break body through middle and pick out meat from joints. Cut with sharp scissors through length of under side of tail, draw meat from shell. Draw back flesh on upper end and pull off intestinal cord and discard. Break large claws and remove meat.

CREAMED OYSTERS

To each 30 oysters use 1 cup thin Cream Sauce, page 35. Drain oysters, saving liquor for soup, put into shallow pan over quick fire and cook about one minute or until edges curl, stirring constantly, and add to sauce.

Or put on oysters with 1 tablespoon butter; add 1 tablespoon flour which has been mixed with a little cold water; add 1/2 cup milk, 1/2 teaspoon salt and 1/8 teaspoon pepper. Worcestershire sauce may be added if desired. Boil 1 minute and serve on thin squares of toasted bread; garnish with parsley.

SCALLOPED OYSTERS

25 oysters
2 cups bread crumbs
1/4 cup milk
2 tablespoons butter
1 teaspoon salt
1/4 teaspoon pepper

Grease dish and cover bottom with bread crumbs, then lay oysters in carefully; season and cover with bread crumbs; pour over milk and cover top with butter. Bake in hot oven 15 to 20 minutes.

FRIED OYSTERS

Wash and drain oysters. Season with salt and pepper, dip in flour, egg and then bread or cracker crumbs. Fry in hot fat until golden brown. Drain well and garnish with lemon and parsley.

CLAM CHOWDER

25 clams
6 potatoes
1 onion
1/8 lb. finely cut salt pork
2 teaspoons salt
1/8 teaspoon pepper
1 quart milk

Chop hard parts of clams. Slice potatoes and onion thin. Put pork into kettle and cook a short time; add potatoes, onion, seasoning and juice of clams. Cook 2-1/2 hours; then add clams. Boil 15 minutes and just before serving add hot milk.

SHELL FISH A LA NEWBURG

2 cups finely cut shrimp, scallops, lobster, or crab meat
2 tablespoons butter
1 tablespoon flour
1 cup milk
2 hard boiled eggs
1 teaspoon salt
cayenne pepper to taste

1/4 teaspoon paprika
1/4 cup sherry

If canned fish is used cover with cold water 20 minutes and drain. Melt butter in saucepan; add flour and stir until smooth; add cold milk slowly; boil until thick. Rub egg yolks through strainer and add, stirring until smooth; add seasoning, and finely chopped egg whites; add fish; put all in top of double boiler over fire for 15 minutes; add sherry and serve immediately.

MEATS

ROASTING

Wipe meat with damp cloth. Trim and tie into shape if necessary. Put some pieces of fat in bottom of pan, and season meat with salt and pepper. Have oven very hot at first and when meat is half done reduce heat. Baste every 10 to 15 minutes. If there is danger of fat in pan being scorched add a little boiling water. Roast from 10 to 15 minutes for each pound of meat, as it is desired rare or well done.

BROILING

The rules for roasting meat apply to broiling, except that instead of cooking it in the oven it is to be quickly browned, first on one side and then on the other, over hot coals or directly under a gas flame, turning every minute until done. Meat an inch and one-half thick will broil in 8 to 15 minutes. Season after it is cooked.

PAN BROILING OR FRYING

Put meat to be broiled or fried in very hot frying pan, with very little or no fat. Turn every few minutes until cooked. Season and serve immediately. Steaks and chops may be pan-broiled without any fat in the pan. For thin gravy pour a little boiling water into pan after meat is taken out.

BOILING AND STEWING

Fresh meat for boiling should be put into boiling water and boiled hard for about 5 minutes; reduce heat and boil gently about 20 minutes for each pound, salt and spices may be added for seasoning. A little vinegar put into the water with tough meat makes it tender. The broth of boiled meat should always be saved for soups, stews or gravies. Salt meats should be put in cold water, which as soon as it boils should be replaced by fresh cold water, repeating if necessary until meat has palatable flavor when done. Salted and smoked meats require about 30 minutes slow boiling, to each pound. Vegetables and herbs may be boiled with them to flavor. When cooked keep hot until required, if they are to be served hot; if they are to be served cold, cool in liquor in which they were boiled. Very salt meats, or those much dried in smoking, should be soaked over night in cold water.

POT ROASTING

Tough cuts of meat may be first browned in fat, then half covered with boiling water and cooked slowly either in oven or in iron kettle on top of stove. This method requires long, slow cooking.

STEW WITH DUMPLINGS

2 pounds lean beef, mutton or veal
1 quart potatoes
2 cups cut carrots
2 cups cut onions
1 cup tomatoes
1 tablespoon salt
1/4 teaspoon pepper
1 tablespoon flour
2 tablespoons chopped parsley

Wipe meat, cut into small pieces, put in kettle, cover with boiling water and boil slowly 1-1/2 hours; add carrots and onions; boil 15 minutes, then add potatoes, salt, pepper and tomatoes; add boiling water, if needed to cover vegetables; boil 30 minutes. Add dumplings and boil 10 minutes without lifting cover. Put meat and vegetables on platter with dumplings around edge. Add flour which has been mixed with a little cold water; boil 3 minutes; pour over stew and sprinkle with parsley.

DUMPLINGS

1 cup flour
2 teaspoons Royal Baking Powder
1/2 teaspoon salt
1 teaspoon shortening
cold water

Sift flour, baking powder and salt; rub in shortening lightly with fingers; add enough water to make dough hold together. Drop by spoonfuls into stew.

LIVER AND BACON

Have liver cut in thin slices; wash, drain, dry and roll in flour. Put bacon thinly sliced into very hot frying pan; turn until brown and transfer to hot platter. Fry liver quickly in the hot bacon drippings, turning often. When done put on platter with bacon. Pour off all but 1 or 2 tablespoons fat, add 1 to 2 tablespoons flour, and stir until brown. Add hot water gradually to make smooth gravy, season and boil 1 minute.

ROAST LAMB

Wipe meat with damp cloth. Put one or two thin slices of onion on top; season with salt and pepper. Put into roasting pan in hot oven and roast for about one hour and a quarter. Reduce the heat after lamb has been roasting about 20 minutes. Serve on hot platter with brown gravy or mint sauce.

ROAST STUFFED SHOULDER OF LAMB WITH BROWNED POTATOES

3-1/2 or 4 pounds shoulder of lamb

DRESSING

2 cups stale bread crumbs
1 tablespoon finely cut onion
1 tablespoon drippings
1 tablespoon chopped parsley
1 teaspoon salt
1/8 teaspoon pepper

Wipe lamb with damp cloth; fill pocket with dressing and sew up. Put into hot oven for 20 minutes. When well browned, season with salt and pepper, add 1 cup cold water and roast 45 minutes; add 1 quart white potatoes, which have been washed, pared and boiled, and roast until potatoes are brown. Remove to platter. Add water to pan to make 2 cups of gravy. Thicken gravy by adding 1 tablespoon flour mixed with a little cold water, season and cook until smooth.

POT ROAST OF BEEF WITH BROWNED POTATOES

Wipe beef with cloth, put into iron kettle or frying pan and brown well on all sides. Add 2 tablespoons cut onion, 1 tablespoon salt, 1/4 teaspoon pepper and 2 cups boiling water; and boil slowly 1-3/4 hours; add water as it boils away, 1 cup at a time. After adding potatoes, boil 30 minutes. Place meat and potatoes on hot platter. Add 1 tablespoon flour mixed with a little cold water to gravy and boil. Pour over meat and sprinkle with chopped parsley. Carrots cut in small pieces may be added with potatoes.

BAKED VEAL WITH TOMATO SAUCE

1 thin veal cutlet
1 teaspoon drippings
1 teaspoon chopped onion
1 teaspoon chopped parsley
1/2 cup bread crumbs
1/2 teaspoon salt
1/8 teaspoon pepper

Trim edge of cutlet and spread on board or platter. Fry onion in drippings until tender; add bread crumbs and parsley mixed with enough water to hold them together; spread on cutlet and roll; tie in three or four places. Dust with salt, pepper and flour. Place in pan; add 1/2 cup hot water. Roast in hot oven 35 to 45 minutes, adding water if needed. Remove to hot platter; pour tomato sauce around meat and garnish with parsley.

VEAL CUTLET

Cutlet may be cooked whole or cut into pieces for serving. Dust with salt, pepper and flour; dip in 1 egg beaten with 1 tablespoon milk, then in bread crumbs. Brown on both sides in shallow fat in hot frying pan. Add boiling water to cover; season and cook slowly for 1 hour. Thicken gravy with 1 tablespoon flour mixed with a little cold water.

ROAST LOIN OF PORK

Wipe pork with damp cloth. Put into pan in very hot oven for 20 minutes, or until well browned, then add 1 teaspoon salt, 1/8 teaspoon pepper and 1 cup cold water. Roast slowly 3 to 4 hours. Add water as necessary. To gravy, add 1 tablespoon flour mixed with cold water, season and boil until thick.

APPLE SAUCE

Wipe, pare and quarter sour apples; remove seeds and core; put into saucepan and add cold water to almost cover. Cook slowly until soft. Add about 1/2 cup sugar for each quart of apples. Cook a few minutes longer; remove from fire; add little lemon peel and serve either hot or cold.

BAKED HAM

Wash and scrub ham in warm water; soak over night. Whether a whole or half ham, put on to boil with cold water enough to cover; boil slowly 4 to 5 hours or until tender, allowing about 30 minutes to the pound. Cool in water in which it was boiled; remove skin carefully; put in pan; cover with 1 cup brown sugar and 1 teaspoon pepper; add 2 cups cold water; bake in very hot oven 45 to 60 minutes; baste often. When brown add 1 cup cider or 1/2 cup vinegar and thicken with 2 tablespoons flour.

CREAMED SWEETBREADS

Lay sweetbreads in cold water with a little salt for 1 hour. Drain, put into saucepan, cover with boiling water and boil very slowly 25 minutes; drain and when cool separate and remove all membrane. Cut into small pieces and reheat in Cream Sauce, page 35.

POULTRY

HOW TO CLEAN

Singe fowl over free flame. Cut off head just below bill. Untie feet, break bone and loosen sinews just below joint; pull out sinews and cut off feet. Cut out oil sac. Lay breast down, make small slit from backbone toward head; loosen windpipe and crop and pull out. Push back skin from neck and cut off neck close to body. Make slit below end of breastbone, put in fingers, loosen intestines from backbone, take firm grasp of gizzard and draw all out. Cut around vent so that intestines are unbroken. Remove heart, lungs and kidneys, wash inside and out with cold water, then wipe dry with cloth. Cut through thick fleshy part of gizzard and remove inside heavy skin without breaking, then cut away gristly part so that only thick fleshy part is used.

ROAST POULTRY

After poultry is cleaned and washed inside and out with cold water, fill inside with dressing. Have at least a yard fine twine in trussing needle. Turn wings across back so that pinions touch. Run needle through thick part of wing under bone, through body and wing on other side; return in same way, but passing needle in over bone, tie firmly, leaving several inches of twine. Press legs up against body, run needle through thigh, body and second thigh, return, going round bone in same way; tie firmly. Run needle through ends of legs, return, passing needle through rump; if opening is badly torn, one or two stitches may be needed; if steel skewers are used put one through wings of fowl and other through opposite thigh. Then wind twine in figure eight from one handle of skewer to other. Rub all over with soft butter and season. Place on rack in roasting pan and put into very hot oven. Make basting mixture with 1/2 cup each of butter and water; keep hot and baste every 10 or 15 minutes. Roast 3 hours for 8 pound turkey, 1 to 1-1/2 hours for chicken and ducks 3 to 4 pounds. If bird is very large and heavy, cover breasts and legs with several thicknesses of paper to keep from burning.

POULTRY DRESSING

2 cups stale bread
1 tablespoon finely cut onion
1 tablespoon drippings
1 tablespoon finely cut parsley
1/2 tablespoon salt

1/8 teaspoon pepper
1/4 teaspoon paprika
powdered sage if desired

Soak bread in cold water 5 minutes and press out all water. Put drippings and onion into pan and cook slowly, stirring constantly, until onion is tender but not brown. Add bread, parsley and seasoning and mix well together.

OYSTER DRESSING

20 oysters
2 tablespoons butter
4 cups bread crumbs
1/2 tablespoon salt
1/4 teaspoon pepper
1 tablespoon chopped parsley

Drain and rinse oysters with cold water. Put butter in saucepan with oysters and bring to boiling point; add bread crumbs, seasoning and parsley; mix carefully, so that oysters will not be broken.

GIBLET GRAVY

Boil neck, gizzard and wing tips together until tender. Pour off excess of fat in pan in which poultry has been roasted; add enough stock from the gizzard and neck to make 3 cups of gravy. Chop gizzard, liver and heart and add; then add 1 teaspoon finely cut onion, 1 teaspoon salt, 1/8 teaspoon pepper, 2 tablespoons flour mixed with a little cold water. Boil 3 minutes.

FRICASSEE OF CHICKEN

Prepare and cut up as for fried chicken. Put into saucepan with just enough boiling water to cover; add a teaspoon salt, a little pepper and, if desired, a teaspoon of onion juice. Boil slowly 2 hours or until tender; add a little water from time to time, as it boils away. Thicken with a tablespoon flour mixed with a little cold water and add a tablespoon of finely chopped parsley. Serve with border of hot boiled rice or dumplings.

FRIED CHICKEN

Singe, wash and clean chicken; cut into pieces as follows: two second joints, two drumsticks, two wings, breast cut into two pieces, backbone cut into four pieces. Wipe with damp cloth; sprinkle with salt and pepper; dredge in flour. Put into frying pan with 2 tablespoons bacon drippings or half drippings and half butter and brown quickly. Add a little water, cover, reduce heat and fry slowly on both sides. Remove chicken; mix 1 tablespoon flour with whatever gravy or fat is in pan; add 1 cup cold milk or water; boil until thick.

CHICKEN PIE

Singe, draw and clean a 4-lb. chicken as usual. Disjoint, cut the breast into four pieces, cut the thigh and leg apart. Save the neck, wing tips, heart, gizzard and liver for soup. Put on the rest with enough boiling water to cover; cook 2 hours.

Add 2 quarts washed, pared and diced white potatoes. Cook 20 minutes, or until the potatoes are tender. Add 1 tablespoon salt, 1/4 teaspoon pepper, 1 table-spoon chopped parsley and 2 tablespoons flour mixed with a little cold water. Boil 3 minutes. Pour all into dish, cover with rich pastry. Bake 20 minutes in moderate oven.

PASTRY

Sift together 1 cup flour, 2 teaspoons Royal Baking Powder, 1 teaspoon salt; rub in very lightly 4 tablespoons shortening; add just enough cold water to make a stiff dough. Roll out on floured board and put over top of pie.

ROAST GOOSE, BREAD AND APPLE DRESSING

Wipe inside with damp cloth, and season with salt and pepper; put in dressing and sew up. Push back skin and cut off neck. In the skin put 2 apples, which have been pared and quartered; tie the skin. Put in pan breastbone up; dust with salt, pepper and flour. Place in hot oven; when browned baste with 2 cups cold water; turn breast side down and roast 2 hours, basting three or four times with cold wa-ter. Ten minutes before serving turn breast side up. Remove fat and make gravy as directed for Roast Poultry.

APPLE DRESSING

1 tablespoon drippings
2 tablespoons chopped onions
1 quart finely chopped apples
4 cups stale bread crumbs
1 egg
1 teaspoon salt
1/2 teaspoon grated nutmeg
1/8 teaspoon pepper
1/8 teaspoon paprika
2 tablespoons chopped parsley

Put drippings and onion into frying pan, cook a few minutes and add apples. Cover bread with cold water a few minutes, remove and press out all water. Put into pan; add seasoning and beaten egg and parsley. Mix well until thoroughly cooked.

FISH, MEAT AND VEGETABLE SAUCES

THIN CREAM SAUCE

1 tablespoon butter
1 tablespoon flour
1 cup milk or cream
1/2 teaspoon salt
1/8 teaspoon white pepper

Melt butter in saucepan, add flour and mix well; add cold milk slowly, stirring until smooth and creamy; add salt and pepper and boil about 3 minutes.

THICK CREAM SAUCE

2 tablespoons butter
2-1/2 tablespoons flour
1 cup milk or cream
1/2 teaspoon salt
1/8 teaspoon white pepper

Make as directed for Thin Cream Sauce.

TOMATO SAUCE

3 slices bacon cut into small pieces
1 slice onion—chopped
2 tablespoons flour
1-1/2 cups strained tomatoes
1 tablespoon chopped green peppers
1/2 teaspoon salt
few gratings of nutmeg
cayenne

Put bacon into saucepan, add onion and brown slightly. Add flour, tomatoes which have been heated, and stir until thick and smooth. Add seasoning and peppers.

BECHAMEL SAUCE

1 tablespoon butter
1 tablespoon flour
1/2 cup thin cream

1/2 cup white stock—chicken or veal
salt and pepper

Melt butter in saucepan; stir in flour; reduce heat; add seasoning and liquid, stirring until smooth.

EGG SAUCE (FOR FISH)

1 cup white sauce
2 chopped hard-boiled eggs
1 tablespoon chopped parsley
1 teaspoon lemon juice or vinegar

Add eggs, parsley and lemon juice to white sauce after removing from fire.

BROWN SAUCE OR GRAVY

1 tablespoon butter or fat in which meat was cooked
1 tablespoon flour
1 cup beef stock or boiling water
salt and pepper

Brown butter in saucepan; add flour and brown; add liquid and stir until smooth and thick. Season to taste and simmer 5 minutes.

CURRANT JELLY SAUCE

1/2 glass currant jelly
1 cup hot brown sauce

Melt jelly over slow fire. Add sauce; stir well and simmer one minute.

HOLLANDAISE SAUCE

1/2 cup butter
2 beaten egg yolks
1 tablespoon lemon juice
salt
cayenne
1/2 cup boiling water

Cream butter; add gradually, stirring well, egg yolks, lemon juice, salt and cayenne; add boiling water slowly. Stir over boiling water till thick as boiled custard. Serve immediately.

SAUCE TARTARE

Make 1 cup mayonnaise, page 41. Chop very fine 1 tablespoon each of capers, olives, pickles and parsley. Press in a cloth till quite dry. Blend gradually with the mayonnaise.

MAITRE D'HOTEL BUTTER

2 tablespoons butter
1 tablespoon lemon juice
1/2 teaspoon salt
1/8 teaspoon white pepper
1 tablespoon chopped parsley

Cream butter; add gradually lemon juice, seasoning and parsley. Keep cold until served.

MINT SAUCE

1/4 cup chopped mint leaves
1/2 cup vinegar
1/4 cup water
1/4 cup brown or granulated sugar

Cook all ingredients in saucepan over very slow fire for about one-half hour. Do not allow to boil. Serve hot.

HORSE-RADISH SAUCE

2 tablespoons butter
2 tablespoons grated fresh horse-radish
1 tablespoon very thick cream
1/2 teaspoon lemon juice

Cream butter; add horse-radish, cream and lemon juice. Keep very cold.

CRANBERRY SAUCE

1 quart cranberries
2 cups sugar
1 cup water

Put all together into saucepan. Cover until it boils. Remove cover and cook about 10 minutes or until berries have all burst. Pour into mold, chill and serve.

For Cranberry Jelly strain and put into mold and chill.

EGGS

BOILED EGGS

Drop into boiling water and boil 3 to 3-1/2 minutes for soft boiled, 12 to 20 minutes for hard boiled; or place eggs in boiling water, cover, and cook over moderate heat without boiling from 8 to 10 minutes for soft, 20 to 40 minutes for hard cooked.

POACHED EGGS

Break eggs and drop carefully one at a time into boiling water in shallow greased frying pan. Cook slowly until eggs are set. Remove each with skimmer and serve on toast garnished with parsley.

POACHED EGGS IN CREAM

Put half cup of cream sauce into shallow baking dish. Open eggs carefully and place on sauce. Cook over boiling water from 10 to 15 minutes or until eggs are set or as firm as desired. Cover with half cup of cream sauce, sprinkle with chopped parsley and dust with paprika and serve.

SCRAMBLED EGGS

Break eggs into bowl, season with salt and pepper and pour into hot frying pan in which butter has been melted. Cook over slow fire and as eggs thicken stir until cooked. If desired eggs may be beaten with milk, cream or water and cooked in same way.

SCALLOPED EGGS WITH HAM

4 hard-cooked eggs
2 cups cold boiled ham chopped fine
1 cup cream sauce
2 cups bread crumbs
2 tablespoons milk

Cut eggs into slices; cover bottom of greased baking dish with one-third of bread crumbs; then add in layers eggs, ham, cream sauce, crumbs, being sure to save bread crumbs to cover top. Add milk and bake in moderate oven 20 minutes.

PLAIN OMELET

Beat 3 eggs with 3 tablespoons milk; add 1/2 teaspoon salt and 1/8 teaspoon pepper, and mix. Melt 1 teaspoon fat in hot frying pan; pour in eggs; lift edges of omelet, allowing thin portions to run underneath, shaking pan until egg is set; when brown underneath, fold over and serve on hot platter.

PUFFY OMELET

4 eggs
1/2 teaspoon salt
1/3 teaspoon pepper
2 teaspoons Royal Baking Powder
1 tablespoon corn starch
1/2 cup milk or half milk and half water

Separate eggs; mix salt, pepper, baking powder, corn starch and milk with yolks of eggs. Beat whites until light though not dry and mix in well with yolks. Put into greased hot frying pan and cook slowly until well puffed up. Dry out in oven, fold over in half and serve immediately on hot platter. If desired serve with tomato sauce, page 35 added before omelet is folded.

FANCY OMELETS

A great variety of omelets can be made by either mixing chopped vegetables, fruits, meats, or shellfish with plain omelet before cooking, or folding them in after cooking.

CROQUETTES

SALMON CROQUETTES

1 cup cooked salmon
1 tablespoon butter
1 tablespoon flour
1/2 cup milk
1/2 teaspoon salt
1/8 teaspoon pepper
1 teaspoon lemon juice

Make a cream sauce with the butter, flour and milk. Put salmon into bowl and add the sauce, lemon juice and seasoning; mix with fork until salmon is well broken. Set aside and when cold mold into desired shapes; roll in bread crumbs, then in egg beaten with 1 tablespoon cold milk, then in bread crumbs. Fry in deep hot fat.

RICE CROQUETTES

1 cup rice
2 eggs
3 tablespoons milk
1 teaspoon salt
1 tablespoon sugar
1 tablespoon butter
1 teaspoon chopped parsley

Wash rice several times and boil with 2 quarts boiling water 30 minutes. Drain well and put into top of double boiler. Add 1 egg beaten with 2 tablespoons milk, salt, sugar, butter and parsley; cook until egg thickens. Cool and shape into cones, balls or oval cakes. Dip into egg beaten up with 1 tablespoon milk. Roll in bread crumbs and fry in deep hot fat until brown.

NUT AND POTATO CROQUETTES

2 cups hot riced potatoes
1/4 cup cream or milk
1/2 teaspoon salt
1/8 teaspoon pepper
few grains cayenne

yolk of 1 egg
1/3 cup chopped pecan nut meats
1/2 teaspoon Royal Baking Powder

Mix all ingredients with fork until light. Shape as for croquettes. Roll in bread crumbs. Dip in egg which has been mixed with a little cold water. Roll in bread crumbs again and fry in deep hot fat until brown. Drain on unglazed paper and serve.

CHICKEN CROQUETTES

2 tablespoons butter
2 tablespoons flour
1 cup milk
2 teaspoons salt
1 teaspoon Worcestershire sauce
1/8 teaspoon paprika
1/8 teaspoon pepper
1 tablespoon chopped parsley
2 cups chopped chicken
2 eggs

Melt butter in saucepan; add flour and cold milk slowly, stirring until smooth and creamy; add seasoning and parsley. Boil 3 minutes. Add chicken; mix well and pour out on platter to cool. When cool enough to handle take a large spoon of the mixture in floured hands; shape into balls, cones or oval cakes and put into cold place until firm. Roll in bread crumbs, then in eggs beaten with 2 tablespoons cold milk, then in bread crumbs. Fry in deep hot fat, and drain on brown paper.

LUNCHEON DISHES

CHICKEN PATTIES

2 tablespoons butter
2 tablespoons flour
1 cup chicken stock
1/2 teaspoon salt
few grains cayenne pepper
1 cup cold diced chicken

Melt butter in saucepan; stir in flour; add chicken stock; season and bring to a boil; add chicken and cook slowly 5 minutes. Fill patty shells and serve at once.

ROYAL PATTY SHELLS

2 cups flour
2 teaspoons Royal Baking Powder
1/2 teaspoon salt
4 tablespoons shortening
ice water

Sift flour, baking powder and salt together; add shortening and rub in very lightly with tips of fingers; add very slowly enough water to make stiff dough. Roll out thin; cut into circles and form on the outside of patty or muffin tins. Bake in hot oven, open side down, until light brown; remove carefully from tins find return shells to oven and bake 5 minutes, open side up.

BOSTON BAKED BEANS

1 quart beans
1/2 pound salt pork
1 tablespoon salt
1/4 teaspoon pepper
1/2 teaspoon dry mustard
2 tablespoons molasses

Wash and soak beans over night. Put half into bean pot; wash salt pork and place in center; add remainder of beans, salt, pepper, mustard, molasses and 4 cups cold water; cover. Put into slow oven and bake 8 hours. Add more water if needed.

BAKED MACARONI WITH CHEESE

1 cup macaroni
1 tablespoon butter
1 tablespoon flour
1 cup milk
1/2 cup grated cheese
1 teaspoon salt
1/8 teaspoon pepper
1/8 teaspoon paprika

Boil macaroni in salted water until soft; drain and rinse with cold water. Put into buttered baking dish and cover with sauce. Cover top with grated cheese and bake 20 minutes in hot oven.

SAUCE

Melt butter in saucepan; add flour, mix well and add cold milk slowly, stirring until smooth; add cheese, salt, pepper and paprika. Boil 2 minutes.

CHEESE IN SCALLOP SHELLS OR RAMEKINS

1 cup milk
2 cups bread crumbs
1/2 teaspoon salt
1/8 teaspoon pepper
1/4 teaspoon Worcestershire sauce
2 cups grated American cheese

Pour milk over bread crumbs, add seasoning, half the cheese and mix well; fill greased scallop shells or ramekins; sprinkle with remainder of cheese and a few fresh bread crumbs and bake in moderate oven 30 minutes.

CHEESE STRAWS

1 cup grated American cheese
1 cup flour
1 teaspoon Royal Baking Powder
1/16 teaspoon cayenne pepper
1/4 teaspoon paprika
1 egg
2 tablespoons milk

Mix together cheese, flour, baking powder, cayenne pepper and paprika; add beaten egg; mix well; add milk enough to make a stiff dough. Roll out 1/4 inch thick, on floured board; cut into strips 5 inches long and 1/4 inch wide. Bake in hot oven 15 minutes.

KIDNEY BEANS WITH BACON

Wash and soak 1 pint kidney beans in cold water over night; drain, cover with boiling water, add 1/4 pound bacon, boil until beans are tender, and drain. Season beans with salt and pepper to taste. Brown thin slices of bacon in frying pan, and serve over beans.

TOMATOES AND EGGS

Grease muffin tins; put one thick slice of unpeeled tomato into each tin; season with salt and pepper; break one egg on top of each slice; again season with salt and pepper and put a small piece of butter on top of each egg. Bake in oven until egg is set but not hard. Serve on rounds of toast and garnish with parsley.

CORN PUDDING

1 quart fresh corn cut from cob
1 teaspoon salt
1/4 teaspoon pepper
3 eggs slightly beaten
2 cups milk
3 tablespoons melted butter

Put all ingredients into greased baking dish and bake in moderate oven until firm.

SCOTCH POTATOES

1 quart potatoes
1 quart onions
1 teaspoon salt

Wash, pare and cut potatoes and onions in half-inch rounds. Put into saucepan with boiling water to cover, adding salt. Boil 25 or 30 minutes, or until tender. Drain, put into dish and cover with Thick Cream Sauce. Bake in hot oven about 25 minutes.

FRENCH TOAST

1/2 cup flour
1 teaspoon Royal Baking Powder
1/4 teaspoon salt
1/2 cup milk
1 egg
sliced bread

Sift together flour, baking powder and salt; add milk and beaten egg; beat well. Into this dip bread, fry in hot fat, drain, and serve hot with powdered sugar.

CHEESE SOUFFLE

2 tablespoons butter
3 tablespoons flour

1/2 cup milk
1/2 teaspoon salt
few grains cayenne
1 cup grated American cheese
yolks of 3 eggs
2 teaspoons Royal Baking Powder
whites of 3 eggs

Melt butter, add flour, and when well-mixed add milk slowly. Add salt, cayenne, and cheese. Remove from fire, add yolks of eggs beaten until light. Cool mixture and mix in baking powder and beaten egg whites. Bake in greased dish 25 minutes in slow oven. Serve at once.

VEGETABLES

Summer vegetables should be cooked on same day they are gathered. Look them over and wash well, cutting out all decayed parts. Always cook vegetables in freshly boiled water and keep water boiling until done. When cooking green vegetables add salt last few minutes of cooking.

Potatoes—Boil 25 to 40 minutes.

Turnips—Boil from 40 to 60 minutes.

Beets—Boil from 1 to 2 hours before peeling.

Parsnips—Boil from 30 to 50 minutes.

Spinach—Boil 20 to 30 minutes.

Onions—Boil in 2 or 3 waters, 45 to 60 minutes.

String Beans—Boil 1 to 1-1/2 hours.

Shell Beans—Boil 30 to 60 minutes.

Green Corn—Steam 10 to 15 minutes, or boil 5 to 6 minutes.

Green Peas—Boil in as little water as possible 30 to 45 minutes.

Asparagus—Boil 20 to 30 minutes.

Winter Squash—Boil 20 to 40 minutes in small quantity of water.

Cabbage—Boil 45 minutes to 2 hours.

ASPARAGUS

Wash, scrape, cut off about one inch hard ends, and tie together. Put into saucepan, cover with boiling water, and boil until tender, keeping tips out of water for the first ten minutes; add salt. Remove from water; lay on pieces of toast and serve with melted butter, cream or Hollandaise Sauce.

PICKLED BEETS

Wash and boil six medium sized beets until tender. Remove skins; slice or cut into quarters; cover with 1/2 cup vinegar, 1 teaspoon salt, 1/8 teaspoon pepper and 1 tablespoon sugar.

CREAMED CARROTS

Wash and scrape carrots; cut into thin slices. Cover with boiling water and boil until tender. Drain and mix with cream sauce or melted butter. Sprinkle with chopped parsley.

BOILED NEW CABBAGE

Cut cabbage into quarters, removing hard part of core, and place in cold water 30 minutes. Drain, cover with boiling water and boil, without a cover, 30 minutes or until tender. Drain, put into dish and pour over Cream or Bechamel Sauce.

COLD SLAW

Wash cabbage; cut into quarters, and then slice very thin; allow to stand in cold water 30 minutes; drain well and cover with boiled or French dressing.

SPINACH

Pick over carefully and wash thoroughly in severed waters until every bit of sand is removed. Put into large kettle and add very little boiling water, about 1/2 cup. Young spinach does not need any water. Boil until tender or about 25 minutes. Drain thoroughly, chop fine and drain again. Season with salt and pepper and garnish with slices of hard boiled-eggs.

CAULIFLOWER

Remove leaves and wash cauliflower; place in uncovered saucepan, stem end down; cover with boiling water; boil 35 minutes or until tender and serve with Cream Sauce.

FRENCH FRIED POTATOES

Pare and cut potatoes into long even pieces. Put into cold water for about an hour. Drain and dry well. Fry in deep fat until brown and cooked through; drain on unglazed paper. Salt just before serving. Sweet potatoes may be prepared in same way.

POTATO CAKES

Pare and boil 1 quart potatoes; mash and season with salt, pepper and paprika; add 1 tablespoon melted butter; mix lightly. Take a spoonful into floured hands and roll. Dip in egg beaten with 1 tablespoon cold milk, then in flour. Fry in deep or shallow hot fat.

BRUSSELS SPROUTS

Wash and cover with cold water for an hour. Drain; put over fire in saucepan of boiling water; boil 20 to 25 minutes without a cover. Drain and cover with cream sauce; or serve with salt, pepper and melted butter.

BOILED CORN

Husk corn, removing all silk. Put corn into fresh boiling water to cover; and boil rapidly for 5 minutes. Remove from water and place on platter on which a napkin has been spread, covering corn with ends of napkin. Serve immediately.

LIMA BEANS

Shell beans just before using. Rinse in cold water. Put into saucepan; cover with boiling water and boil until tender. Drain and add seasoning and melted butter.

KOHL-RABI

Peel turnip-shaped globe; cut into small pieces; boil until tender, 30 to 35 minutes. Add one teaspoon salt to each quart water. Serve plain with melted butter and pepper, or with cream sauce.

The leaves may be stemmed and cooked as greens, boiling 40 minutes.

CANDIED SWEET POTATOES

Boil in salted water 1 quart sweet potatoes until tender; drain and scrape off skins; cut into slices and lay in shallow greased baking dish; brush with melted drippings or butter; sprinkle with 1/2 cup brown sugar; add 2 tablespoons butter. Bake in hot oven until well browned.

BAKED TOMATOES

6 tomatoes
2 cups soft bread crumbs
1/2 teaspoon salt
1/8 teaspoon pepper
1 tablespoon butter

Wash tomatoes and cut off stem ends; remove pulp from center and fill with bread crumbs seasoned with salt and pepper; sprinkle with bread crumbs, and place small piece of butter on each. Bake in hot oven 30 minutes. The pulp may be seasoned to taste, cooked in the pan and served as a sauce.

BROWNED PARSNIPS

1 quart parsnips
1 teaspoon salt
2 tablespoons butter or bacon drippings
1/8 teaspoon pepper

Wash, pare and cut parsnips into 1/2 inch slices. Cover with boiling water and boil until tender, 25 to 30 minutes; drain. Brown on greased griddle or frying pan. Season with salt and pepper.

OYSTER PLANT

Wash and cover with boiling water. Cook 40 to 60 minutes or until soft. Peel, cut in pieces and serve with Cream Sauce.

STUFFED POTATOES

Bake 4 large potatoes. Cut in half lengthwise and, without breaking-skins, scoop out insides and mash; add 1/2 teaspoon salt, 1/8 teaspoon pepper, 1 teaspoon chopped parsley, 1 tablespoon melted butter and mix with fork. Return to shells, put a few drops milk on top; rough with fork; sprinkle with paprika. Place in oven until brown.

SALADS AND SALAD DRESSINGS

All salad greens, such as lettuce, chicory, endive, romaine, or watercress, should be fresh, crisp, dry and cold. Wash leaves carefully and put on ice in lettuce dryer or in cloth.

Dressings wilt the leaves; they should be added just before serving.

Salads may be made in infinite variety. Lettuce plain or combined with vegetables, cold meat, fish, or fruits may be used with French or Mayonnaise Dressing.

FRENCH DRESSING

Put 1 tablespoon lemon juice or vinegar, 1/2 teaspoon salt, 1/8 teaspoon pepper or few grains cayenne pepper into bowl; add 3 tablespoons oil, beating constantly. Serve very cold.

MAYONNAISE I

1 egg yolk
1/2 teaspoon dry mustard
1/2 teaspoon salt
1/16 teaspoon cayenne pepper
1 cup salad oil
2 tablespoons vinegar or lemon juice

Utensils and ingredients should be very cold. Put egg yolk into shallow bowl; add seasoning, mix well; add oil slowly, almost drop by drop, beating until thick. Thin with vinegar; continue adding oil and vinegar until all is used.

MAYONNAISE II

1 egg
juice of 1 lemon or 4 tablespoons vinegar
1/2 teaspoon salt
2 cups olive oil

Put egg with vinegar or lemon juice and seasoning into bowl, beating with rotary egg beater. Add oil a tablespoonful or more at a time, beating constantly. Well covered, this mayonnaise will keep for three or four weeks.

BOILED SALAD DRESSING

1/2 tablespoon salt

1-1/2 tablespoons sugar
1 teaspoon mustard
1/2 tablespoon flour
few grains cayenne
1/2 cup vinegar
2 eggs
3/4 cup milk
1 tablespoon butter or other shortening

Mix dry ingredients in top of double boiler; add vinegar and beaten egg yolks and mix; add milk and butter. Cook over hot water until thick and smooth. Take from fire and add beaten egg whites. Cool and serve.

RUSSIAN DRESSING

Take 1 cup mayonnaise; add 2 teaspoons chili sauce, 1 can pimentos chopped fine, and if desired a dash of grated cheese.

CHICKEN SALAD

1 quart cold boiled chicken, cut into small cubes
1 pint finely cut celery
1 teaspoon salt
1/8 teaspoon pepper
2 hard boiled eggs
2 cups mayonnaise dressing
6 olives

Mix chicken which should be very tender, with celery, seasoning and one egg cut into small pieces; marinate with little French dressing, and let stand in cold place one hour. Serve on lettuce leaves and spread mayonnaise over top. Garnish with olives and remaining egg cut into slices. Dust with paprika.

FRUIT SALAD

1/2 pound Malaga grapes
2 pears
1 grapefruit
1 orange
1 head lettuce

Wash, peel; remove seeds from all fruit; cut grapes into halves, pears in lengthwise pieces, grapefruit and orange into sections; allow to stand on ice. Serve on lettuce leaves with French dressing. Alligator pears, cassaba melon or other fruit may be substituted for above.

VEGETABLE SALAD

1 cup finely cut red cabbage
1 cup cold boiled red beets

1 cup cold boiled carrots
1 cup cold boiled potatoes
1 cup finely cut celery
1/2 cup pimentoes
1 head lettuce
1 cup French dressing

Soak cabbage in cold water 1 hour; drain and add beets, carrots, potatoes and celery. Mix well together, season with salt and pepper and serve on lettuce leaves. On top put strips of pimento and serve with French dressing, to which may be added one teaspoon onion juice.

MARQUISE SALAD

3 firm tomatoes
1/2 cup chopped onion
1/2 cup chopped parsley
2 tablespoons salad oil

Peel tomatoes and cut in half. Mix onion and parsley, add oil; let stand two hours before using. When ready to serve line salad bowl with lettuce, place tomatoes in it and on each half put 1 tablespoon onion and parsley mixture. Pour on French dressing. Everything should be ice cold.

POTATO SALAD

1 quart cold boiled potatoes
1 onion finely sliced
1/2 teaspoon salt
chopped parsley
1/2 cup French dressing

Cut potatoes into slices or cubes; add onion; mix with salt, parsley and French dressing. Serve on lettuce leaves with boiled dressing.

LOBSTER SALAD

Cut cold boiled lobster into small pieces. Marinate with French dressing; put on lettuce leaves; cover with mayonnaise and garnish with lobster claws, olives, hard-boiled eggs and capers.

FISH SALAD

2 cups shredded lettuce
1 can tuna fish or 1-1/2 lbs. any cold boiled fish
1/2 cup French dressing
1 teaspoon onion juice
1/2 cup mayonnaise
1 cup finely cut celery
1 teaspoon chopped parsley

Line dish with lettuce; place fish in center; pour over French dressing to which onion juice has been added and cover with **celery**; put Mayonnaise on top. Sprinkle with chopped parsley.

BEVERAGES

HOW TO MAKE COFFEE

The best method of making coffee, as determined by the Better Coffee-Making Committee of the National Association of Coffee Roasters, is as follows:

"Fill a kettle with fresh cold water and put it on to boil. Place over an open china teapot, kept just for coffee, a clean, wet, old linen napkin, or a new square of unbleached muslin, letting it sag toward the center. Put into the depression 4 heaping tablespoons (for 4 cups of coffee) of finely pulverized coffee. This fine pulverization is very important. Ordinary ground coffee will not do at all, and gives weak infusions.

"When the water in the kettle is boiling fiercely, pour it through the coffee slowly until 4 cups have gone through, or a trifle more for 4 cups of coffee.

"Cover and take at once to table.

"Wash the cloth immediately and keep it in a jar of cold water, never permitting it to get dry, and freshening the water every day. Keeping the cloth sweet is essential. Every effort should be made to this end. The least souring ruins the coffee.

"Follow these directions strictly, paying especial attention to having the coffee very fine, like flour, and the water boiling, and you will have excellent coffee even though you buy cheap blends."

BOILED COFFEE

For 4 cups. Beat half an egg white with 3 tablespoons cold water; add 3/4 cup ground coffee and stir until moistened; put into scalded coffee pot; add 1 quart boiling water and boil 5 minutes. Add 1/4 cup cold water and allow to stand 3 minutes to settle and serve.

COCOA

The usual rule is 2 teaspoons cocoa, 1 teaspoon sugar; 1 tablespoon cold water and 3/4 cup milk to each cup. Mix cocoa with sugar and cold water; cook over slow fire until thick; add milk, and boil 1 minute.

COCOA SYRUP

2 cups water

2 cups sugar
1 cup cocoa
1/2 teaspoon salt

Stir water and sugar in saucepan until dissolved; boil 5 minutes; mix cocoa with cold water to make a paste and add to boiling syrup; boil slowly for 10 minutes; add salt. When cold put into bottle or glass jar in refrigerator. Take 2 tablespoons of syrup for each glass or cup of milk. Serve with whipped cream.

Served either hot or iced, this is a nourishing and delicious beverage.

TEA

Water for tea should be freshly heated and just boiling. Teas are of different strength, but a safe rule is 1 teaspoon dry tea to 1 cup water. Scald teapot; put in dry tea and cover for 1 minute. Add boiling water and cover closely. Allow it to stand 3 to 6 minutes and strain off into a second hot pot.

CHOCOLATE

Cut into small pieces 1 ounce unsweetened chocolate; add 1 tablespoon sugar and 2 tablespoons hot water. Boil all together till smooth; add gradually 2 cups scalded milk; cook in double boiler 5 minutes. If desired add 1/4 teaspoon vanilla. Serve with whipped cream.

CANDIES

CREAM CANDY

2 cups sugar
2 tablespoons vinegar
1 teaspoon lemon extract
1 teaspoon cream of tartar

Add a little water to moisten sugar; boil with vinegar and cream of tartar without stirring, until brittle when tried in cold water. Add flavoring; turn out quickly on buttered plates. When cool enough to handle, pull until white, and cut into pieces.

BUTTER SCOTCH

2 cups sugar
2 tablespoons water
2 tablespoons butter

Boil without stirring until brittle when tested in cold water. Pour out on buttered plates to cool.

BUTTER TAFFY

3 cups brown sugar
1/2 cup molasses
1/4 cup water
1/4 cup vinegar
4 tablespoons butter
1 teaspoon vanilla extract

Boil sugar, molasses, water and vinegar. When crisp in cold water add butter and cook 3 minutes. Add vanilla and cool on buttered pans and break into pieces.

CHOCOLATE CARAMELS

2 cups molasses
1 cup brown sugar
1 cup cream or milk
1/4 pound unsweetened chocolate
4 tablespoons butter

Put all ingredients into kettle. Boil until it hardens in cold water; add 1 teaspoon vanilla and turn into greased tins. When nearly cold, cut into small squares.

CREAMED NUTS

2 cups confectioner's sugar
white of 1 egg
1 teaspoon vanilla extract
2 teaspoons cold water
walnuts or other nuts

Mix sugar, unbeaten egg white, vanilla and water into a stiff paste. Shape into little balls, press between halved walnut or other nut meats.

Stoned dates and large seeded raisins may be filled with this cream, or it may be mixed with chopped nuts, shaped into bars and cut into squares.

PEANUT BRITTLE

2 cups chopped roasted nuts
3 cups granulated sugar

Put sugar in frying pan. Stir over slow fire. It will lump, then gradually melt. When pale coffee color, and clear, add nuts and pour quickly on greased tin. When cold break into pieces.

CANDIED POPCORN

1-1/2 cups sugar or maple syrup
1 tablespoon butter
3 tablespoons water
3 quarts popped corn

Boil sugar or syrup with butter and water until it spins a long thread; pour this on corn and if desired shape into balls.

PULLED MOLASSES CANDY

1 cup molasses
2 cups brown sugar
1 cup water
3 tablespoons vinegar
3 tablespoons butter

Put molasses, sugar, water and vinegar into saucepan and stir; boil until very brittle when dropped into cold water; add butter and pour on buttered platter. When cool enough to handle, butter hands and pull until light brown. Pull into oblong strips and cut with scissors.

FUDGE

3 cups sugar

1 cup milk or cream
4 or 5 tablespoon's cocoa or 2 ounces unsweetened chocolate
1 tablespoon butter
1 teaspoon vanilla extract

Put sugar, milk and cocoa or chocolate into saucepan; stir and boil until it makes soft ball when tested in cold water; take from fire, add butter and vanilla, cool and stir until creamy. Pour on buttered plates and cut into squares.

PENUCHE

2 cups light brown sugar
1/3 cup milk or cream
1 tablespoon butter
3/4 cup chopped nuts
1 teaspoon vanilla extract

Put sugar, milk and butter into saucepan. Boil with as little stirring as possible until it makes a soft ball when tested in cold water. Take from fire; add nuts and vanilla; beat until thick and pour into greased tins.

COCOA CREAM CANDY

4 tablespoons confectioner's sugar
2 tablespoons boiling water
4 tablespoons cocoa
1/2 teaspoon vanilla extract

Mix sugar and water until smooth; add cocoa and vanilla; mix until creamy. Dust hands with sugar; take up 1/2 teaspoon of mixture and roll into ball. Dust a plate with sugar, and lay balls on to dry about 2 hours; then roll in finely chopped nuts.

STUFFED PRUNES OR DATES

Wash, dry and stone fruit; cut almost in half and fill with a half marshmallow or blanched almond, or chopped nuts and raisins and roll in sugar.

COCOANUT CREAM CANDY

1 tablespoon butter
3/4 cup milk
2 cups sugar
1/2 cup grated fresh cocoanut
1/2 teaspoon vanilla extract

Melt butter in saucepan; add milk and sugar; stir until sugar is dissolved, heating slowly; boil 12 to 15 minutes; remove from fire and add cocoanut and vanilla, beating until creamy. Pour into buttered tins and cool.

For Chocolate Cocoanut Cream Candy add 3 ounces unsweetened chocolate to other ingredients before boiling.

HICKORY NUT CANDY

2 cups sugar
1/2 cup water
lemon or vanilla extract
1 cup hickory nut meats

Boil sugar and water, without stirring, until thick enough to spin a thread; place saucepan in cold water; add flavoring and stir quickly until white; stir in nuts; turn into buttered tin; when cold cut into squares.

DATE AND PEANUT PASTE

1 cup stoned dates
1/2 cup peanut butter
1 teaspoon salt
1/4 cup confectioner's sugar

Wash and dry dates; put through food chopper; add peanut butter and salt. Mix and roll into small balls; then cover with sugar. Lay on plate to dry.

SALTED ALMONDS

Blanch almonds by putting into boiling water for a few minutes. Remove skins, dry well and brown in heated olive oil or butter in pan on top of stove stirring continually. Take from fire when very light brown, as they continue to color after removing from pan. Drain well on brown paper and sprinkle with salt.

FIRELESS COOKERY

The Fireless Cooker has become an important factor in the home. The principle employed is the preservation of heat by the use of non-conducting materials. The device ordinarily used is a rectangular box lined on all sides with some substance which will prevent escape of heat, with spaces or wells for the insertion of stone or metal discs or radiators and vessels containing food to be cooked.

Among the advantages of this method are: the improvement in flavor by slower cooking with little opportunity for evaporation; improved appearance of food that is subject to shrinkage when cooked by ordinary methods; saving in labor, as the cooking practically takes care of itself. Dinner may be prepared in the morning, placed in the cooker, and without further attention be ready to serve at any time after 3 or 4 hours. While the time required for cooking is longer than in the usual methods, the actual time consumed in preparation of a meal is considerably reduced.

DIRECTIONS

Prepare food for cooking as usual. Place in special vessel, designed to fit into wells of Fireless Cooker, and heat on range or over gas flame until ordinary cooking temperature is reached. Put into cooker with one or more radiators which have been heated for 10 or 15 minutes over hot fire. For roasting, radiator should be hot enough to brown a pinch of flour immediately. Close cover, fasten lightly so that the steam may escape and allow cooking to proceed for time specified in recipes.

For baking cake, apples, etc., proceed as for roasting. The time required for baking is slightly longer than that specified for regular ovens. For cake ordinarily baked in a moderate oven, heat radiators hot enough to brown a pinch of flour in half a minute.

The Fireless Cooker is especially convenient for the preparation of cereals, meats, vegetables and other dishes that are ordinarily boiled or roasted. Remember that foods should be thoroughly heated before putting into cooker.

CEREALS

Prepare cereal for cooking in double boiler as usual. Boil over fire for 5 minutes; place in larger vessel of boiling water in cooker and allow it to remain 4 or 5 hours or longer. If placed in cooker at night it should remain warm enough to serve for breakfast.

STEAMING

For recipes see "Boston Brown Bread," "Steamed Fig Pudding," "Poor Man's Pudding," "Christmas Plum Pudding," etc. Prepare and mix ingredients as directed. Put into greased molds and place in shallow pan of boiling water over very hot radiator in cooker. Fasten cover tight and cook for 5 to 6 hours.

SOUPS

Place ingredients in vessel; cover with cold water; bring to boil over free flame and boil 5 minutes. Fasten cover and transfer to cooker, using one hot radiator in bottom of well. Cook 3 or 4 hours and season when ready to serve.

For ingredients and special directions for preparing soups, see "Soups."

ROAST MEATS

Prepare and season meat in usual way. Place in large dry vessel; put very hot radiator in bottom of cooker well; place vessel containing roast on radiator, and place another very hot radiator on top. Close cooker and fasten. Allow it to remain about one-half hour per pound of meat.

The roast may be browned in a very hot oven before putting into cooker or just before serving.

BOILED OR STEWED MEATS

Prepare meat for cooking as usual, searing in frying pan if desired brown. Place in large vessel and cover or partly cover with boiling water, boiling with cover fastened tight for 10 or 15 minutes over free flame. Transfer to cooker, using one hot radiator underneath. Cook 2 or 3 hours, season and serve.

VEGETABLES

Prepare vegetables as usual. Place in vessel with small quantity of boiling water. As there is little evaporation in fireless cookers, allowance does not have to be made for loss by evaporation. Boil over free flame for 5 to 10 minutes. Transfer to cooker, using one radiator in bottom of well. Cook 3 or 4 hours, remove from cooker, season and serve.

INVALID COOKERY

Always prepare food for the sick in the most careful and attractive manner. In sickness the senses are unusually acute and far more susceptible to carelessness and mistakes in the preparation and serving of food than in health.

BARLEY WATER

2 tablespoons pearl barley
2 quarts cold water

Wash barley, soak several hours in cold water and boil gently in same water for 2 hours; or put into double boiler and cook for 4 hours or until reduced one-half. Lemon juice and sugar or salt to taste may be added if desired.

PINEAPPLE JUICE

Peel a very ripe pineapple, cut into small pieces and put through fruit press or potato ricer to extract all juice. Strain and serve with cracked ice.

ALBUMINIZED ORANGE

1 egg white
juice of 1 orange
sugar

Add orange juice sweetened to taste to egg white and beat well. Chill on ice and serve cold.

BEEF TEA

1 pound lean beef
1 cup cold water

Cut beef up into small pieces or put through meat chopper. Put into fruit jar; add water and allow to stand 15 to 20 minutes to draw out the juice. Place on trivet or rack in pan of cold water; heat very slowly for about 2 hours. The water must not boil. Season, strain, cool and remove fat. Beef tea may be served hot or cold.

SCRAPED BEEF

Scrape meat with sharp knife from lean beef cut from round until nothing but connective tissue is left. Form into small balls and broil slowly for about 2 minutes. Season and serve. For sandwiches do not cook but spread between thin slices of bread and season.

SPANISH CREAM

    2 cups scalded milk
    4 egg yolks
    1/4 cup sugar
    2 tablespoons granulated gelatine
    1/4 cup cold water
    1 teaspoon vanilla extract
    1 pint cream

Pour scalded milk very slowly over egg yolks and sugar which have been mixed together. Cook slowly in double boiler until thick and smooth. Pour over gelatine which has been soaking in 1/4 cup of water. Chill, add vanilla and beat with egg whip until thick. Add the cream which has been whipped and chill in molds.

GLUTEN MUFFINS

    2 cups gluten flour
    3 teaspoons Royal Baking Powder
    1 egg
    1 tablespoon butter
    2 cups milk

Sift together flour and baking powder; add beaten egg and melted butter to milk and add, Mix well and bake in greased muffin tins in moderate oven about 35 minutes.

In addition to the foregoing, many of the soups, broths, jellies, ices and plain drop cakes found in the preceding pages are suitable for invalids and convalescents.

PRESERVING AND CANNING

(Material adapted from U. S. Food Administration and N. Y. State Department of Agriculture.)

GENERAL DIRECTIONS

Test all jars for leakage before using. To do this, fill with water, put on rubber and cover, seal and invert.

Sterilize all utensils, jars, covers, etc., by covering with cold water, and boil for 10 minutes. Use only new rubbers and dip in boiling water just before using.

Use a wide-mouthed funnel when filling jars to avoid loss of material and keep jar rim clean.

Invert all jars after filling and sealing.

Fruit should be sound, firm and not overripe. All fruit should be carefully prepared.

Clean fruit, clean hands, clean utensils, and a clean kitchen free from flies, are essential for safety and success.

Keep products in a cool place. Avoid freezing in winter.

CANNING

Canning is the operation of preparing sterilized food so that it will keep indefinitely.

The custom of canning fruit in syrup is based on the improvement in flavor and texture which sugar gives to fruit. Sugar is not necessary for its preservation. Success depends upon thorough sterilization—that is, killing the organisms which cause food to spoil, and then sealing carefully to prevent their entrance. Fruit may be canned in water, in fruit juice and in syrup.

PRESERVING

The only difference between preserving and canning fruit is that sugar is always used in preserving, while in canning it is used in smaller quantity or not at all. In preserving the old rule of equal weights of sugar and fruit may be followed.

DIRECTIONS FOR CANNING BY OPEN-KETTLE METHOD

By this method which is generally used, for preserves, jams and marmalades, food is completely cooked and poured boiling hot into sterilized jars.

Prepare fruit, which may or may not be peeled, and cut into pieces depending on the variety. Blanch or scald peaches and similar fruits to loosen skin and chill by plunging into cold water. Cook slowly in as little water as possible or in fruit juice or fruit syrup until done. Fill the sterilized jars, seal and invert.

DIRECTIONS FOR CANNING BY CAN-COOKED METHOD

By this method uncooked or partly cooked food is packed in can or jar, covered with liquid and both jar and contents sterilized.

Pare fruit if desired or blanch or scald in boiling water a small quantity of the fruit at a time. (See time table.) Do not blanch cherries, sour cherries excepted, berries or plums.

Chill outside of the blanched fruit by immersing it for a few minutes in a vessel of cold water. Remove skin from such fruits as peaches.

Pack firmly in clean, tested jars to within one-half inch of top.

Fill jars to within 1/4 inch of top with boiling water, fruit juice, or syrup.

Place a new rubber on each jar, adjust cover and partly seal.

Place jars on false bottom of water bath and sterilize for required time. (See time-table.) If the hot-water bath is used, jars should be immersed in sufficient boiling water to cover tops to depth of about 1 inch. Do not begin to time the sterilizing until water boils. Keep water boiling during sterilizing period.

Remove jars from sterilizer. Seal them and invert to cool. Avoid a draft on jars, but cool as rapidly as possible.

Wash and label jars. Wrap in paper or store in a dark place to prevent loss of color of red fruit.

Vegetables may also be canned by this method.

A TIME-TABLE FOR CANNING FRUITS BY THE CAN-COOKED METHOD

TIME OF COOKING			
	Time of Blanching	If the hot-water bath is used	If the Pressure Cooker is used (5 Pounds)
FRUIT	Minutes	Minutes	Minutes
Apricots, Peaches	1-2	16	10
Blackberries		16	6
Cherries, Strawberries, Grapes, Plums	16	10	
Fruit Juices		20	10

Huckleberries, Rasp-berries		16	8
Pears	1-2	20	10
Pineapples		60	40
Quinces	1-2	60	40

USE OF SUGAR IN CANNING FRUIT

Sugar is used in canning fruit for the purpose of improving flavor and is not necessary for preservation.

Thin syrup—1 part sugar to 2 parts water for sweet fruits.

Medium Syrup—1 part sugar to 1 part water for berries and medium sweet fruits.

Thick Syrup—2 parts sugar to 1 part water for sour fruits.

To make syrup add sugar to boiling water. Stir until all sugar is dissolved, then boil 2 or 3 minutes.

CANNED PEACHES

Scald sound, firm freestone peaches, a small number at a time, in boiling water just long enough to loosen skins; dip them quickly into cold water and slip off skins. Cut peaches in halves, and remove stones. Have ready a syrup made by boiling sugar and water together until sugar has dissolved, using 1/2 to 3/4 cup sugar to each cup water. Allow about 1 cup syrup for each quart jar of peaches. Put in 1 cracked peach pit for every quart of syrup.

Can-cooked Method.—Pack peaches in overlapping layers with rounded side uppermost and blossom end facing glass. Fill each jar with hot syrup and adjust rubber, cover and upper clamp, thus partly sealing jar. Place jars on a rack in hot water to cover tops to a depth of 1 inch. Bring water to boiling point, and boil pint jars 16 minutes, quart jars 20 minutes. Remove jars, seal and invert to cool.

Open-kettle Method.—Cook peaches in syrup until tender; then with sterilized spoon slip them carefully into sterilized jar; fill jar to overflowing with syrup. Adjust rubber, cover, seal immediately, and invert to cool.

CANNED CHERRIES

Wash. Cherries should be pitted before being canned in order to conserve space. Can sweet cherries as berries. Blanch sour cherries 1/2 minute, in boiling water. Dip in cold water; drain and pack closely into hot sterilized jars. Cover with boiling water or boiling medium syrup. Loosely seal. Sterilize 16 minutes in boiling water bath. Remove jars at once, tighten covers, invert to test seal and cool.

CANNED PEARS

Wash and peel fruit and follow directions for canned peaches.

CANNED BERRIES

Blackberries, blueberries, huckleberries, raspberries, loganberries, gooseberries and strawberries should be canned as soon as possible after picking. Hull or stem; place in strainer and wash by lifting up and down in pan of cold water.

Pack into hot sterilized glass jars, using care not to crush fruit. To insure a close pack, put a 2 or 3 inch layer of berries on the bottom of jar and press down gently with spoon. Continue in this manner until jar is filled. Boiling water or boiling thin or medium syrup should be poured over the fruit at once. Loosely seal. Sterilize 16 minutes in boiling water. Remove jars, tighten covers, invert to test seal and cool.

ASPARAGUS

Asparagus for canning must be fresh and tender. Select tips of uniform size and maturity and wash. Cut into lengths according to containers to be used. Scrape off scales, tough outer skins and hard ends and tie in bundles large enough for one jar.

Immerse the lower ends in boiling water and leave them immersed for 5 minutes, then the entire stalks, leaving them in 1 to 3 minutes longer.

Cold dip, drain, pack neatly, tips up, in hot sterilized jars. Add salt and cover with boiling water. Loosely seal, sterilize two hours in boiling water bath. Remove as soon as time is up. Tighten covers, invert to test seal and cool.

BEANS

Green String Beans and Wax Beans.—The beans should be tender and fresh, and graded according to size and washed. Leave whole or break in uniform pieces. Blanch 5 to 10 minutes until the pod will bend without breaking. Cold dip, drain well and pack into hot jars. Add salt and cover with boiling water. Loosely seal and sterilize two hours in boiling water. Remove when time is up, tighten covers, and invert to test seal.

CORN

Make careful selection of tender, juicy sweet corn, at best stage for table use. Can as soon as possible after gathering. Remove husks and silk; blanch tender ears 5 minutes, older ears 10 minutes. Cold dip and cut from cob but not too close. Pack at once into hot sterilized jars. As corn swells during sterilization, leave space of 1 inch at top. Add salt and cover with boiling water. Be sure that water penetrates through corn to the bottom of jar. Loosely seal and sterilize three hours in boiling water. Remove when time is up, tighten covers, invert to test seal and cool.

JAMS

Jams are usually made with small fruits or with chopped large fruits. Cook slowly with an equal weight of sugar until thick; put into sterilized tumblers or jars and seal.

RASPBERRY JAM

Pick over berries. Mash a few in bottom of preserving kettle; continue until fruit is used. Heat slowly to boiling point and add equal quantity of heated sugar. Cook slowly 45 minutes. Put into sterilized jars.

Blackberry, gooseberry or other berry jam may be made in this way.

PLUM CONSERVE

4 pounds plums
1 cup seeded raisins
2 oranges
sugar
juice of 1 lemon
1/2 pound walnuts

Wash plums; remove stones; add raisins and oranges which have been sliced very fine. Measure and add 3/4 cup sugar to each cup fruit and juice. Put into kettle, cook slowly about 45 minutes or until thick like jam, stirring to keep from burning. Add lemon juice and chopped nuts. Pour into sterilized jars.

SPICED CURRANTS

3 lbs. white sugar
5 lbs. ripe currants
1 tablespoon cinnamon
1 tablespoon nutmeg
1 tablespoon cloves
1 tablespoon allspice
1/2 pint vinegar

Boil currants one hour, then add sugar, spices and one-half pint vinegar, boil one-half hour longer. Pour into jars and store.

JELLIES

Heat and mash fruit until juice runs readily. If fruit is not entirely broken up rub through coarse sieve. Pour into sterilized jelly bags of unbleached muslin or doubled cheesecloth and drain thoroughly but do not squeeze. Take 7/8 cup sugar for each cup of juice. Boil juice 8 to 20 minutes (berries and currants less than other fruits); add sugar which has been heated in oven; stir until sugar is dissolved and boil about 5 minutes. Pour into hot sterilized tumblers. Hard fruits like apples and quinces should be cut up, covered with cold water and cooked until tender before turning into jelly bags.

PICKLES

PICKLED PEACHES

2 pounds brown sugar
2 cups vinegar
1 ounce stick cinnamon
1/2 ounce whole cloves
4 quarts peaches

Boil sugar, vinegar and spices 20 minutes. Dip peaches quickly in hot water; then rub off the fuzz with a cloth. Place a few peaches at a time in syrup and cook until tender. Pack into sterilized jars. Adjust sterilized rubbers, and fill each jar to overflowing with hot strained syrup. Put on sterilized covers and seal jars immediately.

CHOW CHOW

1 quart small white onions
1 quart small cucumbers
2 heads cauliflower
3 green peppers
1 quart vinegar
6 tablespoons mustard
3 tablespoons flour
1 cup sugar
1 tablespoon turmeric

Peel onions and add cucumbers, cauliflower cut into small pieces, and sliced peppers. Soak over night in brine (1 cup salt to 1 quart water). Drain and cook in fresh brine until vegetables are tender, and drain again. Boil vinegar in kettle and add paste made with mustard, flour, sugar, turmeric and a little cold vinegar, stirring until mixture thickens; add vegetables and cook slowly 10 minutes. Seal in sterilized jars.

SWEET TOMATO PICKLES

1/2 peck green tomatoes
4 onions
4 green peppers
1 cup salt

1/2 cup white mustard seed
2 teaspoons pepper
3 teaspoons cinnamon
3 teaspoons allspice
3 teaspoons cloves
2 quarts vinegar
1 pound brown sugar

Chop tomatoes, onions and peppers; cover with salt and allow to stand over night. Drain, and add to vinegar, spices and sugar which have been heated to boiling. Cook 15 minutes and seal in sterilized jars.

CHILI SAUCE

12 medium-sized ripe tomatoes
1 red pepper
1 onion
2 cups vinegar
1/3 cup sugar
2 tablespoons salt
2 teaspoons cloves
2 teaspoons cinnamon
2 teaspoons allspice
2 teaspoons nutmeg

Peel and slice tomatoes; add chopped pepper and onion; put into kettle with remaining ingredients. Cook slowly for 2-1/2 hours. Seal in sterilized jars.

TOMATO CATSUP

4 quarts tomatoes (strained)
6 tablespoons salt
3 tablespoons black pepper
1 tablespoon cloves
2 tablespoons cinnamon
2 tablespoons allspice
1-1/2 pints vinegar

Put all together in kettle and boil down one-half. Pour into sterilized jars.

KEEP THE HOME BAKING SAFEGUARDED

Housekeepers who have always used Royal Baking Powder with utmost satisfaction are sometimes misled into experimenting with baking powders containing questionable ingredients.

No real economy is thus accomplished—in fact, the use of an unwholesome, undependable baking powder often produces a bitter taste in the food which makes it unappetizing and sometimes inedible, to say nothing of the injurious effect produced upon the digestive system.

Royal Baking Powder is most economical. Its well-known dependability makes baking success simpler and surer, thus preventing loss of eggs, flour, butter and other ingredients. Only the best materials are used in its production—pure cream of tartar and tartaric acid, derived from grapes, bicarbonate of soda and corn starch, all scientifically blended and perfectly balanced. The best is always the most economical.

To insure food that is always delicious, wholesome and appetizing, insist on using Royal Baking Powder which is made from Cream of Tartar, derived from grapes.

BAKE IT WITH ROYAL AND BE SURE

has been the motto for fifty years in millions of homes where good food is recognized as the first essential of good health and where pride is taken in good baking.

One of the distinctive qualities of food baked with Royal Baking Powder is *wholesomeness*.

This is health insurance of such vital importance that millions of women bake at home just to be sure that Royal Baking Powder is used.

Remember the adage—

"Bake it with Royal and be sure."

INDEX

C

G

H

S

Lector House believes that a society develops through a two-fold approach of continuous learning and adaptation, which is derived from the study of classic literary works spread across the historic timeline of literature records. Therefore, we aim at reviving, repairing and redeveloping all those inaccessible or damaged but historically as well as culturally important literature across subjects so that the future generations may have an opportunity to study and learn from past works to embark upon a journey of creating a better future.

This book is a result of an effort made by Lector House towards making a contribution to the preservation and repair of original ancient works which might hold historical significance to the approach of continuous learning across subjects.

HAPPY READING & LEARNING!

LECTOR HOUSE LLP
E-MAIL: lectorpublishing@gmail.com